Alive Character Design

Character Design
Course by Haitao Su

Alive

For Game,
Animation and Film

Character

Haitao Su
Vincent Zhao

Design

CYPI PRESS

CONTENTS

FOREWORD

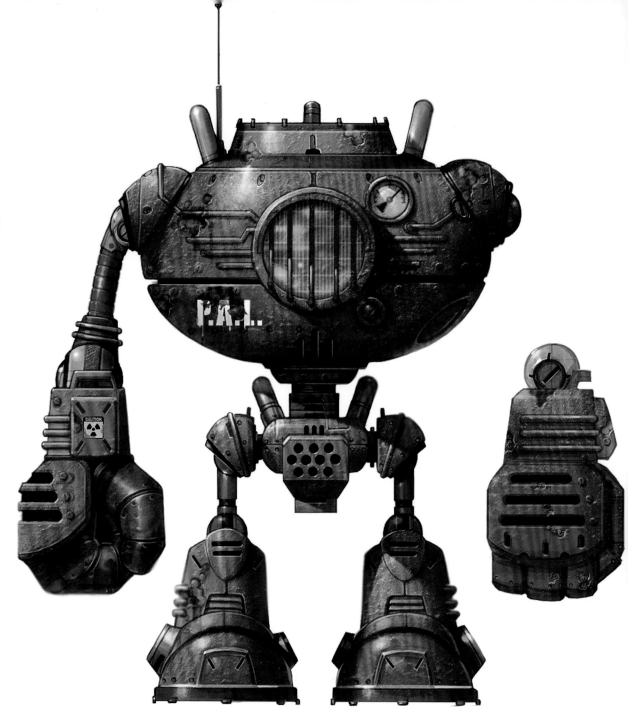

Here I want to extend my sincere thanks to those who have encouraged and helped me in this book! Without them, there would not have been this book! The original inspirations for this book occurred to me around five or six years ago, when my wife found herself in a dilemma of career choices. I spent the entire weekend drafting for her an article on how to become a professional painter. This article was mainly concerned about what preparations are required of an illustrator. But I uploaded this six-page-long manual to the website without much consideration, it turned out to be expectedly popular. The webpage was passed on to more and more people, and some friends started to come to me with relevant questions via email. When I look back, it dawns upon me that this book actually evolved from the article. Though crude, the words turned to be impressively practical out of care for my family. It was then due to the recognition from others that encouraged me to put what I have in mind to paper. Following this anecdote, I started to work on several "brochures" on cartoon illustrations out of interest. I refer to them as "brochures" because they were neither bar-coded nor priced. But thanks to the beauty of digital printing, they have ended up as something that one can pocket and read at any time. Later, one of them — "*The Art of Galactic Bowling*," which only has twenty-two pages, interested a publishing house. An updated version of this brochure is the one you are holding in hand, which is an ideal textbook on character design which one should read from page to page from time to time.

For several years in my prime time, I had my beloved drawing pens covered with dirt. During these years, I was going all out for the magazine "*Fantasy*." Even now, I can declare with the utmost pride that it was the first magazine in China themed on illustrations. Though it only survived for four years until the publication of the forty-ninth volume, both its readers and I myself have learned a lot. From Norman Rockwell the Respectable to Frank Frazetta the Great, their names made frequent presence in the magazine. Through interviewing them, I finally came to the understanding that techniques were not all that matters in painting. In the three years, we had interviewed over a hundred big names in the painting, illustration and cartoon industries. It is my biggest honor to have befriended my idols. The experience that these talented artists had shared with me worked more than all the knowledge I had obtained in my college years and acted as the most practical manuals that one cannot access through college studies. It does sound a little weird, but I did have made improvements in paintings in a rapid way during the several years I had put down my drawing pens. Now, my dear friends, I want to share with you my concept development techniques, digestions and most importantly, the treasured experience. Through this book, I want to thank Peter De Sève the Outstanding, those who have tried their best to offer help and support to "*Fantasy*" as well as those talents who had received our interviews. Though some of you have already dropped out of contact, and that I have no confidence that all of you can happen to come across these words, I am still eager to express my sincere thanks.

Like most "bookaholics," ardent love for books is inherent in us. It is not that we can access knowledge through books; it is that they have facilitated a journey to explore the unknown. Today, online downloading has challenged the prevalence of books considering that many materials can be downloaded from the webpage. However, I still believe that the data which can be copied for an indefinite number of times are never able to hold candle to the fragrance of the printing ink. Upon my entry into the painting domain, referential books on illustration are rarities, while books on character design had not come out yet. In this context, I was so fortunate that I had come across a copy of "*Figure Drawing*" by Andrew Loomis. I was totally drowned in this book. One might well say that this book has made a change to my life. Though

I had no intention to compete with the master and idol in terms of knowledge and skills, I was still obsessed with the ambition to author a book which will be of practical importance to others. This is no longer the case. Nowadays, you will run across hundreds of titles on cartoon and animation in the section of teaching materials in the bookstore, or while searching on the Internet. However, it is a common understanding that these books differ little with each other considering that most of them are concerned with similar CG techniques, which is really misleading. Some beginners in this profession might come up with a false assumption that character design is all about learning CG techniques. As long as someone can use Photoshop or Painter, there is no doubt that he can end up with satisfactory characters for commercial projects. On the contrary, the books that are really worth purchasing are not common at all. Some classical foreign textbooks are still helpful to refer to now and then, even though some contents are already outdated. The list includes Andrew Loomis' series, Burne Hogarth's series, and Christopher Hart's series on animation characters, which are relatively recent. All these books have profound and lasting influence over those committed to this profession.

Though I am as passionate as those talented artists in learning, it is still challenging for me to wrestle with words. In most occasions, I prefer drawing three illustrations to typing down one hundred words. Therefore, this book is illustration-oriented, rather than text-oriented. Fortunately, this orientation happens to appeal to readers of this age, who favor illustrations over texts. As mentioned in the passages above, I hope to give full expression to the experience and digestions from years of practice in the commercial domain of character design. It is expected that the readers will come to understand that character design is not only about CG techniques, but depends on the most efficient and innovative concepts. This profession does not involve repetitive labor, or painstaking skill training. Rather, it allows adventure and creation. Thus, we should prioritize learning and understanding in terms of concepts, and this process itself is a journey which overflows with fun and joy. What readers can obtain from this book is not only how to design characters, but also how to develop

their creative thinking in character design. An outstanding character designer must be eternally interested in novel things. Those copycats will never understand what creation is essentially about. Through years of experience in his industry, it has been evidenced that no copycat can outlast the original artist. Because with the changes in external factors such as environment, no one can take on others' individuality and distinctive styles through purchasing or mimicking activities, or reproduce others' success. However, the original style and feature can get improved and perfected through industrious studies. Therefore, this book is not concerned with some definite rules, but some suggestions and case studies that one can refer to during their studies. I will consider the book a success if it can help the readers to embark on a correct route from the very beginning. It should also be remembered that artists should always choose a path less travelled, which is of paramount importance to character design as one of the overarching rules.

As mentioned in the passages above, character design does not solely depend on drawing techniques. Therefore, I have not talked too much about techniques except in the second chapter, which touches upon the processes in drawing. This is because I want to make a difference from other textbooks that only tell you how to do it rather than why to do it. It is impossible to cover all the relevant points concerning character design. Fortunately, this defect is counterbalanced by a wealth of exquisite illustrations. Even though I cannot act as an impartial judge when it comes to my own works, I still want to highlight that all the illustrations except those in the history section and the gallery part are my own originals, most of which I have produced for commissioning clients. To do this book, I have created or sorted out nearly five hundred illustrations. Some of them have not made way into this book due to the limitation of space. I still hope that I can finish this book with ease, just like I did several years ago.

Haitao Su
Harbin, September 2010

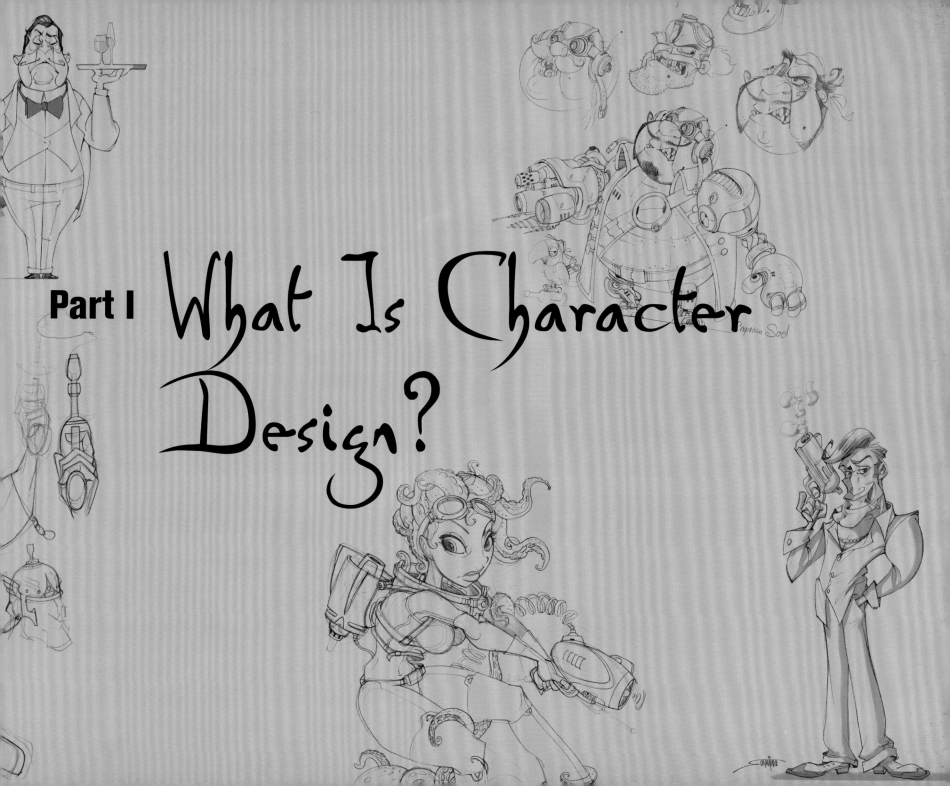

Part I What Is Character Design?

Armed with a piece of white paper, a pen, and coupled with your imagination, you will come up with an impressive character design illustration. But if you want to make illustrating what you live on and live for all your life, how beautiful the illustration looks is not all that you should be striving at and concerned about.

What Is Character Design?

> **"** *As a character designer, it requires more than profound expertise and common sense. A character designer is supposed to be curious and observant. When you approach life as an artist, you will be amazed how interesting everything has become.* **"**

What is character design? This is not a question in a strict sense. Sometimes a certain image just pops out in our mind. Sometimes, we scribble a figure on paper. All these can be called "character design." However, these random scribbles are far from professional works, considering that no one will define them from a professional perspective. In fact, even among those engaged in this profession, not all of them can claim that they truly understand the essence of "character design," or have full confidence that they are professional character designers.

　　This book is intended to illustrate my interpretations of "character design," and share with the readers what I have learnt through two decades of work. I believe that the book will be of considerable help for both the readers and myself.

A tribute to Norman Rockwell from the heyday of American illustration industry

1. What Is Character Design?

We have come back to this question. In simple words, character design is to design human or humanlike characters of distinctive uniqueness and rich features for all kinds of visual media. If this definition still seems a little general, we can deconstruct this term and interpret it as: designing looks and bodies for characters, along with their hairstyles, costumes and props. But this only provides a basic definition. If you want to sound more professional, the definition should be more detailed. A professional character design scheme generally requires the artist to draft the front, back, and side view of the character, the front, side and 3/4 side view of his head, as well as various motions such as walking, running and jumping, in addition to different facial expressions. The application area for character design has expanded from story and movie to animation, cartoon, game, online animation, TV animation, commercials, mascot, illustrated books, model and other visual domains celebrating creativity.

What kind of character will impress the audience in a profound way?

2. What Does a Character Designer Do?

Character designers might be esteemed and envied for their profession. This profession will rank high considering the intensive potential and decent salary. Besides, character design is also one of the most challenging and innovative professions. In the project, a character designer is required to play multiple roles as the director, dresser, lighting engineer, photographer, hair stylist, costumer, props master, and even action choreographer or visual effect artist. Therefore, in the domain of cartoon and animation, a character designer is not only supposed to serve as an actor with pen in hand, but also to act as a casting director as in the movie industry to handpick all the cast. He is a marvelous magician who can infuse vitality to the otherwise inanimate pictures with magical drawing pens. In this sense, he does deserve the appellation of "God," who is able to create everything one can name. Therefore, a character designer has to be curious of anything, and observe all the things around him in addition to possessing adequate expertise and necessary common knowledge. On the other hand, when common people start to observe the life in an artist' perspective, they will find that everything has become intensely interesting.

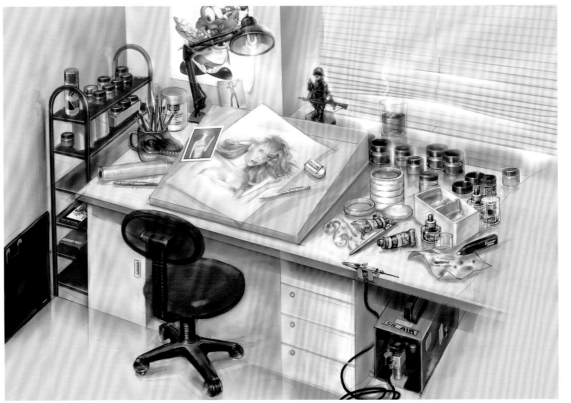

My illustration studio

3. Some History You Should Know

An outstanding character designer is always capable of finding inspiration from ordinary and prosaic things. An understanding of the character design history will help to capture creative inspirations from the impressive oeuvre of those marvelous designers. The one-century history of animation art, the five-century of cartoon art and the history of painting which dates back to the birth of mankind is a reservoir of materials and resources.

In retrospect of human character history, we can put aside the totem and fresco on the cliffs by our ancestors in the ancient times, and skip masterpieces by Leonardo de Vinci and Michelangelo Buonarroti, and go straight to the illustrations in the sarcasm and humor magazines which experienced independent development towards the end of the nineteenth century, which was the origin for the cartoonist characters of our age.

In 1894, "*New York World*" has commissioned R. F. Outcault to author a cartoon column in its Sunday edition to serialize the anecdotes of a boy in yellow night robe from the slum, which might be the first oeuvre of character design. This boy was later enshrined as the first cartoon character in the United States and was affectionately referred to as "the Yellow Kid." Consequently, its creator Outcault was esteemed as the father of American cartoons.

Cartoons came to be prevailing in the publishing industry when it was realized that a fictive character can be so vivid and well-received. In 1898, Michelin Man came into being and achieved great success, crystallizing wide imagination of the Michelin Brothers and talented poster designer Marius Roussillon.

Since then, character design has become more and more active in animation, cartoon and other industries. In 1914, Winsor McCay launched a cartoon movie called "*Gertie the Dinosaur*" featuring storytelling, challenging the established assumption that cartoon is nothing but

Humor and satirical magazines by the end of the 19th century

1898 Michelin Poster © MICHELIN

Michelin Poster © MICHELIN

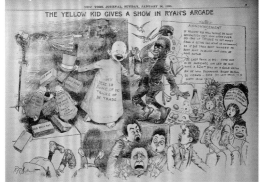
The Yellow Kid © Richard Felton Outcault

The Yellow Kid © Richard Felton Outcault

The Yellow Kid © Richard Felton Outcault

a high art notion. Meanwhile, the ingenuous dinosaur named Gertie became a household name at that time. In 1917, Felix the Cat from a cartoon film produced by Pat Sulivan came into highlight and famed as "a black cat walking on his own." This lonely but cynical black cat has demonstrated Sulivan's impressive imagination, determining the glorious success of this film. In the following sixteen years, Sulivan has finished over one hundred cartoon movies starring Felix the Cat, making it one of the best in the history. In 1928, Walt Disney produced the first sound motion cartoon film called "*Steamboat Willie*," whose leading character is Mickey Mouse. This character marveled the whole world as the trademark of character design for its extensive influence and high returns.

The success of Mickey Mouse heralded the prosperity of the Disney Empire, evidencing that original characters promise indefinite commercial values. Then comes his

partner Donald Duck, who refuses to spend any minute in silence and seems to have difficulty controlling his temper. Due to confidentiality policies, Carl Barks who created Donald Duck remained unknow to fans until his retirement in 1965. Disney has magnetized a large number of talented character designers from all over the world. They are not only focused on producing original characters, but also on renovating the classical characters. They have scored accomplishments in both areas.

In December 1937, Walt Disney Company launched "*Snow White*" based on Grimm's fairy tale, which was the first full-length animated film in history. In

Felix the Cat © Felix the Cat cartoons

Donald Duck © Disney / Carl Barks

Mickey Mouse and Steamboat Willie © Disney

Gertie the Dinosaur © Winsor McCay

Donald Duck © Disney / Carl Barks

Donald Duck © Disney / Carl Barks

this film, Snow White is a thorn in the flesh of her step-mother because of her breath-taking beauty. The evil woman has sworn to put her to death by any means. As the first full-length animation in the world, the success of "Snow White" emblematized Disney's golden days. As an Oscar winner, this film was inscribed into AFI's "100 Years….100 Movies" List. Thanks to the unique concepts, the seven dwarfs in this film are defined by distinctive characteristics as a crystallization of the designers' wisdom and creativity.

Character designers are inspired by things or figures in folk tales or real life. One of my favorite animation characters is Dennis the Menace, who made a debut on "Post-Hall Syndicate Sundays" on March 12th, 1951. The readers have fallen in love with this clever boy ever since, and this image has survived for half a century. This naughty devil who seems unlikely to grow up can always make people laugh in one way or another. The success of this film had also brought fame and fortune to Henry King "Hank" Ketcham, who had based this character on his four-year-old son.

Some classical characters can even define a social or cultural phenomenon and influences people's life. Alfred E. Neuman of the "MAD" Magazine is one of them. He is distinguished by freckles, a missing front tooth and a mischievous face. Nowadays, he has already become the mascot and icon for "MAD" which is the most renowned humor magazines in the US. He is a household name in his country and has never drifted out of the sight of American citizens since his debut on the cover of the 29th Edition of "MAD" in 1955, while his signature phrase "What-Me Worry?" is a common saying among the American public.

Dennis the Menace © Hank Ketcham Enterprises, Inc.

Dennis the Menace © Hank Ketcham Enterprises, Inc.

Snow White and Seven Dwarves © Disney

Alfred E. Neuman © E.C. Publications, Inc.

With the development in the game industry, character designers have new playgrounds. The prosperity of online games has given rise to a public assumption that all the character designers make big money. Names such as Super Mario Bros, Lara Croft, and Shunrei are commonly known. Some games even provide the players opportunities to design their own characters. It is said that the development and prosperity of any profession are pillared by considerable economic strength. All the character designers can put their hearts in their stomachs because their jobs also promise impressive financial gains and enormous development potential. On June 16th, "Toy Story 3" which had been distributed worldwide by Disney/Pixar had earned over 100 million US dollars around the world as the seventh film boasting a box-office exceeding 100 million US dollars in history. It was estimated that Walt Disney Company had taken in 240 million US dollars annually from Toy Story merchandise. Enormous financial support has already taken effect. Character design is concerned with personal creativity as well as cooperation of the entire production team. A certain production staff member is only a certain link of this industrial chain, which means that this creative industry promises enormous opportunities, and that character designers are confronted with unprecedentedly high standards. The ability to draw beautiful characters is far from enough to make a competent character designer. A professional designer is supposed to be distinguished by unique styles and features, which is one of the overriding principles in character design.

Toy Story 3 © Disney

Toy Story 3 © Disney

4. The Overriding Princple in Character Design

In the last century, commercial advertisements, animation, comic, game and other industries have undergone rapid development, which has resulted in the evolution of character design into an independent industry. Industrial demand has led to a rapid development in this industry. Many fresh faces will make debut in this industry every day. Some of them are remembered thanks to their unique characteristics and the designer's creativity, while most of them will fade in our memory because they are dull and boring. As an independent artistic domain, character design features an independent development trajectory, and observes distinctive creative principles. No matter which medium is employed and what changes have taken place, "to highlight the uniqueness" will always play an overriding role in character design. Yes. It's true. As long as a certain character is visually distinctive, it is successful.

Vincent Woodcock remarks in "*How to Draw and Paint Crazy Cartoon Characters: Create Original Characters with Lots of Personality*," "what we need is not a duck, a charming girl or a talking tree. We need uniqueness." How clever he is!

Who said I was not Personalized!

Has this "*Mona Bean-sa*" made you smile?

5. Categories of Character Design

In terms of subjects, character design involves several categories. Characters belonging to the same category are certain to share some common features, while those of different categories will exhibit varied or even contrasting characteristics. For example, cute characters and monsters as a result of genetic variations are just the opposite of each other. Of course, some characters might be defined by more than one kind of features. Evil aliens from outer space are both beasts and villains. No matter whether such categorization holds water, it will help us to have a good understanding of characters in the learning process. Therefore, we will talk about how to deal with female characters, male characters, cute characters, monsters, animals, supporting roles, villains, the inanimate and mechanical characters respectively in the third chapter. In addition, varied categories also differ in terms of the medium to be used. The following passages are concerned with some common categories which I have frequently dealt with. This categorization is intended to facilitate a better understanding of the characters themselves. Generally speaking, there is no definite boundary for a certain category. In comic, cartoon, film, and game, all the characters in a certain work are on the same footing for being equally complicated or uncomplicated, because any disparity might result in a sense of incoherence. However, recent products have challenged this rule. For example, "*Shrek*" has combined a realistic-style princess, a complicated-style Shrek, an ordinary-style donkey and a logo-style talking cookie. This movie has taken advantage of these contrasts to be as satirical as possible by defying the conventions.

Every creative process involves pain and joy.

A **Logo-style:** this category of characters is mostly simplistic. Most of them are cute, with big eyes, small noses or no nose at all, and are used as mascots for public welfare undertakings and commercial campaigns.

B **Simple-style:** this category is more complicated than the logo-style, though following the simplistic approach as well. It performs well in flash promotion and expanded application in newspapers, comics, Internet or TV.

C **Ordinary-style:** as the most common category, it celebrates the animation or cartoon styles. This category is associated with a richer variety of expressions, and is suitable for media such as animation and cartoon which highlight sense of humor and exaggeration.

D **Complicated-style:** the proportion and expressions of such characters are closer to reality despite some exaggerative and comic elements. This category is commonly used in Disney movies and those produced by other animation giants, because it will impress the audience more than the simple-style in an easier way.

E **Realistic-style:** this category is closest to reality and is commonly found in Hollywood blockbusters and high-definition games. It is intended to amaze the audience or players with a sense of reality.

Logo-style

Simple-style

Ordinary-style

Complicated-style

Realistic-style

Part II Basic Principles and Procedures of Character Design

A successful work of character design should not be evaluated on how beautiful it looks. The overarching benchmark is whether it can demonstrate the character's attributes and spirits. If the designers can incorporate their distinctive understanding of a given character into the configuration through the process, this character will never fade in the audience's memory.

Basic Principles and Procedures of Character Design

> " *Outstanding painting skills do help to enhance the visual appealingness of the character. However, a really innovative illustration of character design crystallizes the designer's years of practice, and depends on how the designers are passionate about this artistic domain.* "

Character design is a creative profession that is challenging in a considerable way! Just enjoy it!

At present, it is believed that all the readers have comprehended what the character design is and some milestones marking its evolution history. However, history is all about the past. There is just no point talking too much about it. Sitting back at your desk, you have to depend on yourself to work, or continue with some established procedures. In this chapter, some suggestions concerning character design will be offered, illustrating what it takes to produce works of innovative ideas and impressive quality in my opinion.

Generally speaking, every character designer is supposed to start with the concept development process, and then proceed with the drafting, selecting certain schemes based on communication and negotiation with the clients, coloring and elaborating until the work is finished. The procedure seems predetermined, without much possibility for change or challenge. However, whether a designer can come up with characters of unique properties is not predetermined. What he ends up with might just be the opposite of what he expected.

Outstanding painting skills do help to enhance the visual appealingness of the character. However, a really innovative illustration of character design crystallizes the designer's years of practice, and depends on how the designers are passionate about this artistic domain.

1. Get Yourself Fully Prepared

① Tools

A pencil, a piece of paper, plus your imagination, are all you need to produce an outstanding work. The key to success is not determined by what tools are used by whom. I do believe in this. However, tools of high quality can help to enhance the quality of the finish, save time, and generate your interests and confidence in illustrating. Professional tools, though expensive, are worth every penny you spend on them. In a long shot, expensive tools of high quality are more economical than those that are cheap but crappy.

Lamp: Eye-protection lamp of sufficient illumination and no strobe

Eyes: sharp eyes of acute observation

Patience: ability to hold back from being hasty and edgy
Perseverance: immunity to negative emotions such as frustration and lack of confidence

Propelling pencil: some people prefer propelling pencils because they need not spend time sharpening pencils.

Rubber: used to erase incorrect lines on paper

Pencil sharpener

Pencil sharpener: this kind of pencil sharpener with a handle can easily sharpen the pencil.

Pencil: one that can draw flowing lines without any blur

Mind: skipping in an agile way like a rabbit

Coffee: a cup of coffee brimming over with happiness and sense of success

② Sketch Book

It is common to neglect the importance of sketch books. Many tend to seize the printing paper or any other paper at hand to capture the inspirations flashing by in their minds, considering it a waste to use sketch books for random scribbles. It is advised that they should start to put down their ideas in the sketch books. After a while, these sketch books will become a precious treasure for them. A single sketch book has showcased the drafts and sketches crystallizing their design concepts, as well as some undeveloped ideas and thoughts. It can serve as a time capsule. Every page can revive your memory of what happened back then and how it inspired you. When the designer is working on a certain commission, this sketch book will turn into a bank of brilliant ideas. The designer does not need to rack their brains for ideas, or worry about whether he will turn out to be a copycat. Depending on his sketch book, the designer can make sure that his concept is original. Of course, the designer should take note of the reserve in his bank from time to time.

I'm sorry to say that unlike my foreign counterparts, I cannot open up the sketch book and come up with a sketch in no time. It takes a lot to make it happen. Therefore, the drawings in my sketch book are mainly based on the pictures popping out on the Google webpage. The designer can also train themselves to capture screen shots in videos. In order to create characters featuring distinctive characteristics, one of the key points is to search for inspirations day to day.

The designer is advised to develop a habit of drawing drafts in a sketch books. I've found that many designers like drafting on any paper they can easily lay hand on. In this way, many concepts of incredible values will be gone with the paper, which is an enormous loss as time passes by.

My own sketch book

③ Sources of Inspirations

In fact, creative inspirations can come from everything in daily life. Curiosity coupled with acute observation will generate surging inspirations. Some of the methods covered in the following passages will be a magical remedy for those readers complaining of having exhausted their inspirations.

ⓐ Book and Magazine: Many illustrated books or artistic albums are highly inspirational. A certain page might stir your interest and trigger some brilliant ideas. Even magazines which you use to kill time might enlighten you in some way. The key is that you must take down innovative ideas in an immediate way in case they are needed in the future.

ⓑ Movie and TV: These video media are particularly effectively in exciting brain cells. It must be admitted that Hollywood blockbusters are very influential on those engaged in the creative industry at our age.

ⓒ Sketch Book and Scrapbook: Every designer is supposed to equip himself with these two items. A pocket sketch book can enable the designer to take down what he has just seen and heard at any time. As for the scrapbook, the designer can construct an e-version in his computer, laptop, or even iPad. To establish a meticulous catalogue in the e-scrapbook is of high importance to a designer.

ⓓ Museum and Exhibition: Visiting museums and exhibitions will give a designer the opportunities to have an extensive knowledge of the world and thus broaden his own vision.

ⓔ Internet: Internet might be a late invention compared with the aforementioned media. However, it has already become an indispensable tool for me to collect referential materials and search for inspirations. Using search engines such as Google and Yahoo in an experienced way and defining the search range with clear indexes will enable the designer to find what he has been looking for in a rapid and straightforward way without missing any useful information. Precision search will help to shorten search time by defining the file format.

A collection of masterpieces

Scrapbook and folder for temporary storage

Collections of works and drafts by masters, classical animation works, professional magazines and journals, as well as reference albums and textbooks for artists all construct stairs leading to success.

Musée du Louvre, Paris/Archivio IGDA, Milano/G.Dagli Orti 355

Have you ever taken a serious thought how those big names in the arts domain can inspire you? The illustration shows how I was inspired by Ingres' masterpiece "*The Spring*." Some might be concerned that they will be branded as "copycats" if they have referred to the classical works in their design. Actually, a competent designer can still come up with refreshing and innovative ideas on basis of the classical as a crystallization of human civilization.

2. Basic Processes in Character Design

① Thinking — Asking Yourself Some Questions

"You did see it. But you didn't make careful observation."
— Arthur Conan Doyle in *A Scandal in Bohemia*

What does it take to do character design? The answer is simple — a pencil, a piece of blank paper, as well as a concept of the designer.

Yes! It's true that nothing seems difficult. However, if you really want to be deemed as a professional character designer, it is advised that you should think about this question in a serious way. If asked to depict this process in just one word, I will choose "thinking." Just like what we did in the exams back at school, a designer should learn to understand what he is expected to do in the first place to obtain a profound understanding of the clients' requirements and thoughts and save trouble for the later processes. This might be a golden rule for those experienced designers who are able to finish a project in a swift manner. At this stage, a designer should read the script at a desk in a patient way, striving to analyze what is special about this character. Before initiating the production process, the designer should have already asked himself the following questions:

> Which category does this character belong to?
> What's unique about this character?
> Who are his friends or enemies?
> What will happen to this character?
> What changes will happen to this character at last?

Therefore, character design is not solely based on wide imagination. In most cases, you need to learn from Sherlock Holmes for his sharp eyes and observed thinking. Even though you might still be unsure about the character after answering all these questions, you will not be confused where you should be heading for at least.

Thinking is a habit every character designer must have!

② Draft — "Nail Sketch" of Great Values

As a pre-production phase, the sketching process cannot be the longest one. However, this process is essential for the finish. In order to cultivate a good habit, I will divide this process into three stages.

Stage One: Generally speaking, I will draw some drafts measuring 3 cm to 6 cm in length or width, which I refer to as "nail sketch." Its merits are evident:

a. Small drawings make it easier to identify whether there is anything inconsistent with the overall action;

b. It is easy to find whether the outline of the character is clear enough.

c. Due to its tiny size, the designer can finish it in a short time by following their instincts, which are very important for this process. Designers will always find it impossible to reproduce the nail sketch as the instincts have already gone.

d. The most important thing is that this nail sketch can help avoid obsession with details.

The first stage is intended to explore all the possibilities for inspirations. No matter there are ten, twenty, or fifty proposals, the designer is supposed to put them down on paper one by one. There is no point considering the feasibility issue, as it is what should be done in the next stage.

The second stage involves selecting flexible proposals. The selected proposals should be consistent with requirements and logic, easy to capture and rich in distinctive features and creative ideas. Generally speaking, I will select two to five proposals for elaboration and draw meticulous drafts on A4-size sketch books based on them. At this stage, I will also refer to some pictorial references in depicting the details. The drafts are only intended to capture simplified images. They are still open to revisions. Thus, precision is not required.

The third stage is to scan the finished drafts, and make revisions in Photoshop by adjusting color gradation and deleting the unwanted dot. Save the revised image file in the JPG format (the index should be eight to ten). RGB mode and gradation can also be used, but CMYK format is not recommended, which will lengthen the transfer time due to its big size, and cause color deviation when common image-viewing software are used. The file is supposed to measure 600 to 1000 in pixel. Files featuring higher resolution will take long time to transfer. Besides, people without credibility might take the advantage to use the high-resolution picture directly without informing you.

A nail sketch is small in size but highly useful.

③ Software — A designer should know about unique features of other softwares in addition to the one he's familiar with.

In the passages above, we have talked about what tools are needed for character design. A character designer does not have to obtain a profound and extensive knowledge of software. It is no more than one of the tools, whose performance is determined by the user's competence. However, a designer is advised to grasp either Photoshop or Painter. Artrage and Alias SketchBook of Autodesk are also recommended for substitution. Both softwares are easy to learn.

Software	Company	Merits	Operating System	Notes	Price	Latest Version
Adobe Photoshop	Adobe	Even though Photoshop was originally intended for processing images, it plays a leading role in drawing. Adobe has a defining effect on many drawing software. In these software, layer, channel and filter plug-in are all defined in the Photoshop framework. For those determined to become a professional CG artist, Photoshop is a must.	Windows & Mac	Used to set up the layer format.	490.00 USD	Photoshop CS5
Corel Painter	Corel	Painter is currently the most powerful "natural media" in the world. It is the first one to incorporate traditional drawing methods and computer design, producing distinctive and impressive effects.	Windows & Mac	–	339.00 USD	Corel Painter 11
ArtRage	Corel	ArtRage is a designer for drawing oil paintings. Its functions to emulate drawing pens are powerful in an astonishing way, inferior to no large-scale drawing software. Its interface is highly user-friendly. Even the beginners will find it easy to use.	Windows & Mac	Compatible with user-defined drawing pen, texture, layer and importing functions of PSD file	40.00 USD	ArtRage 3.0
Autodesk SketchBook Pro	Autodesk	As a natural media software from a new generation, this software features uncomplicated interface and outstanding performance to emulate handmade drawing. Autodesk is a giant in industrial design. SketchBook Pro can be used to capture screen shots at a click and add notes through layer, highly recommended for drawing drafts.	Windows & Mac	Compatible with T I F , BMP, GIF, PNG Or JPEG files	89.99 USD	2010
openCanvas	Portal Graphics	OpenCanvas is a Japanese product smaller than 2MB in size, called "OC" for short. When using this tiny CG painting software, the designer will feel as though drawing on paper. Besides, the user can also video his creative process through this software.	Windows	Compatible with drawing pen, brush, layer, filter and selection functions. The latest version is equipped with twenty-two-format layer and more filters.	6,800.00 JPY	openCanvas 4.5
Paint Tool SAI	Systemax Inc.	This 2MB-software is almost a simplified version of Painter. Like other Japanese software, it is user-friendly, and compatible with poorly-equipped computers. There will be no pause even when the big brush is used. SAI is user-oriented, with outstanding performance in line drawing. It is also effective to avoid errors caused by shaking hands. The users can rotate the picture to a certain perspective at their will.	Windows	–	5,250.00 JPY	Ver. 1.1.0

④ Proposal Discussion — Tactics to Negotiate with Clients

A designer can take an upper hand in face-to-face discussions to seize the opportunities to sell his proposal. However, if only email is used, he must come up with a brief, clear and non-confusing presentation. Generally speaking, the clients are likely to make a response one or two days after receiving the drafts. My clients are mostly based in the Western Hemisphere. Therefore, I have chosen to send them the drafts at night, when it is their working time. They will usually give me feedbacks through email before leaving the office. In this way, I can find their feedback in my email box the next morning.

If you have done a good job in the former processes, the clients are highly likely to find the proposals they like from your drafts. If this does not happen, do not push the clients to make selections from the existing proposals. It is not a wise move considering that the clients will start to question your competence and ethics when they have found out that you are only interested in their money. In order to avoid triggering their resentment, you should put yourself in their shoes and try to be as patient as possible. You should understand that all the rejected proposals are not a waste. They have helped you to capture what the clients are really looking for. Mission accomplished! For new clients, it is advised to exceed their expectations by setting up a higher requirement for yourself. In most cases, my clients will not have any question with my works after two or three times of cooperation.

All the drafts act like stairs leading to the finish.

⑤ The Finish — It can be either accepted or rejected

Whether you have done a good job in the former processes determines how long it takes the clients to make a decision on the draft. Experienced designers will find that efforts spent on pre-production thinking, analyzing, drafting and communicating are highly rewarding, considering that the proposal will stand a better chance to be accepted. In this sense, it is the most efficient approach. Of course, if the designer is poorly-prepared, both sides will find it boring and dull due to painstaking communication.

If you have found yourself in such an unfortunate situation, you should avoid any conflict with the clients. No matter how brilliant your proposal is, the clients will reject it in a resentful way, which will cause big trouble. In this situation, you should strive to put an end to the confusion. The optimal solution is to be frank and admit to the clients that you have neglected some considerations in the first place, and then review their requirements in a serious way. Make sure to fully demonstrate your competence in the alternative plan.

Initial concepts will not survive to the very end. However, it does not mean that these drafts have wasted your time. Drafting is a key transitional process. A fantastic finish is built on inspirations from every former stage. At least, you will have a clear idea of what the clients dislike through these stages. All the drafts will act as a touchstone.

Drafts, finish and referential pictures
for character design

⑥ Coloring

At this stage, the production process is close to conclusion. The following process only requires a serious and patient attitude. This chapter is not primarily concerned with color. However, we still need to cover some essential points. First of all, all of us should extend our sincere thanks to the computer for having made things so easy. Though hand-drawn paintings still occupy a prominent position even today due to their uniqueness, the computer has made enormous contributions as a designing and drawing tool considering that it has greatly shortened the coloring time and allowed for indefinite possibilities for revision. In the early years of my career, the clients' decision to change the color sounded like a nightmare for all the designers. Computer has provided a remedy for this. With some understanding of the software, we can shorten this process to a great extent by depending on some simple techniques.

Ⓐ Fill the background layer with the dominant hue, and use gradation to produce a darker color. Drawing on this base color will save time in the coloring process.

Ⓑ Produce light and shade effects by applying different gray scales and then start the coloring process with the "color" function of the coloring brush. In the coloring process, the designer only needs to consider the color factor and think of light and shade effects in the drawing process. He is not required to take two considerations at the same time. Adjusting the color takes the same process.

Ⓒ Use large brushes for base color, and then select smaller corresponding brushes for details.

Ⓓ Some specially-defined brushes can be used to finish coloring certain objects in a quick way, such as the clouds drifting in the air and the flourishing trees.

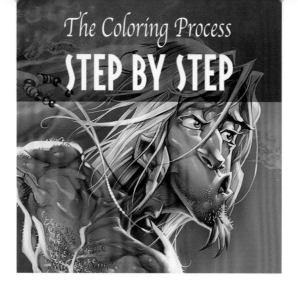

The Coloring Process
STEP BY STEP

❶ Scan the sketches in the sketch book. I like using gradation tools in Photoshop to transfer the sketch into a combination of white base and black lines and then move the black slider on the left of the gradation to the right, because lighter lines can be easily covered in the coloring process.

❷ Set up a new layer after making divisions through magic band. Fill each section with different gradations. The designer should not take care to avoid applying the same gradation to the bordering parts. At last, change the layer attribute into "multiply" as shown in the illustration. At this stage, the character's skin, hair, and shorts have been distinguished out with various gradations.

❸ The beauty is that the designer can use "magic band" to select any division at any time. Now, we can use the "color range" function in the menu to access any division through this gradation layer.

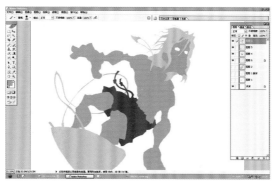

❹ Set up a new layer, and select a color to apply to the existing divisions.

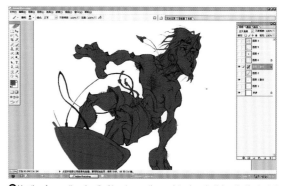

❺ Use the aforementioned method to set up another gradation layer. I will draw the illuminated part on this gradation layer and then again access the illuminated division through color range.

❻ After painting the illuminated part on the gradation layer with the drawing pen, the designer should lock the layer before the coloring process in case that the drawing pen will exceed the selected area. It is advised to use a lighter gradation when painting the illuminated part to make it easier to produce different divisions by avoiding excessive use of gradations.

❼ The designer is supposed to keep the whole picture in mind when painting the illuminated part, without being distracted by details. The finish has a printmaking effect. Elaboration of details is accomplished in the following processes.

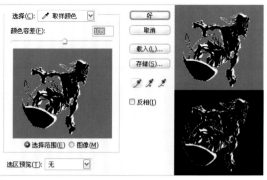

❽ Shut down other layers, only revealing the gradation layer with illuminated parts. Use the "color range" tool in the menu to access the corresponding divisions.

❾ Select the partly-colored layer, and fill the division with bright yellow.

❿ Reduce the transparency for the layer of the pencil drafts to 50% (obscurely visible) so that the outline can be covered up in the elaboration process.

⓫ At this stage, we will start to elaborate on the details. Facial expressions come first so that the designer can fully commit themselves to the most important part, which will help to enhance his own confidence and ensure a good beginning for his works.

⓬ When working on the facial expressions, there is no shortcut. The designer can only depend on acute observation and years of experience.

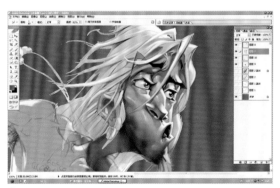

⓭ At this stage, the designer is supposed to start working on the base color. Generally speaking, the designer should finish applying the base color in the initial stage so that he can refer to the color now and then when drawing the characters in the later process. This illustration is an exception. As it is concerned with surfing, we must choose waves as background.

⓮ Before drawing waves, I have used a picture from the Internet to see how it looks.

⑮ At this stage, we will start to focus on the details of the characters when there is no big problem with the base color. Elaborate on the color of different parts one after another, and work on the waves in the background when the characters are finished 70 to 80%, because the designer has to refer to the color of the waves to finish the rest.

⑯ The designer should pay extra attention when drawing the sea due to the unique quality of water. It is transparent, but not colorless. The designer also has to take consideration of reflections and shades. It has a considerable volume, but no definite shape. Therefore, the designer should depend on daily observation experience when painting the sea.

⑰ . We should take a comprehensive analysis and be patient when drawing the sea, because it is so difficult to capture in a precise way. We should make intensive observations of the photos downloaded from the Internet.

⑱ We should start with the reflections of the character and his surfboard, which should be darker than the neighboring objects. The shades basically have the same shape with the reflections. However, the outline will turn ragged because of the reflective effects. Meanwhile, due to the influence of waves, there is a gradation of color within the reflections.

⑲ Due to the reflective effects on the water surface, light purple will be used to capture what it looks like when the warm color of midday sunshine meets the cold color of the sea water. In order to illustrate the glittering waves, the designer is supposed to select the "color filter" function of the brush, which will produce a desired effect.

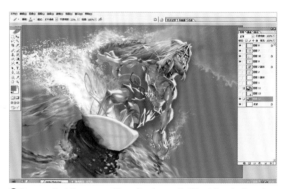

⑳ The sprays due to the pressure of the surfboard come at last. Due to the refraction and reflection effects, waves have turned nearly white like the sunshine rays. Here, we can enlarge and color the sprays in the picture to finish the background.

㉑ Re-trim the character's edge and his outline bordering the background. As the divisions were defined by using tools such as magic band, it was not precise enough, which means that we need to make further efforts in this stage to make adjustments. In this process, the designer has to check how the big picture looks from time to time.

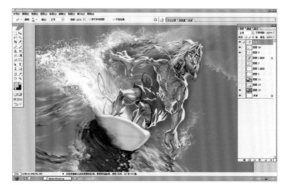

㉒ Add highlight and blink, check the reflections, and deal with the relationship between the major character and the background in terms of light and shade. In order to give prominence to the character, I usually adopt the Rembrandt-style lighting approach, which involves deepening the background at the character's outline in the foreground, while increasing the luminance of the background on the darker parts.

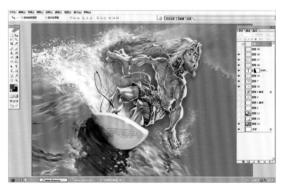

㉓ Draw the patterns or logos on the shorts and surfboard. Afterwards, the designer can sit back and savor the joy. The sense of success will act as a motivation for the next illustration.

⑦ Making Revisions — Putting a Perfect Conclusion

The final phase is about making certain revisions on the basis of the color sketch. In this stage, the designer has to spend more efforts on observation, instead of making revisions with drawing pens. In the production process, 40% time is intended for drafting and selecting the drafts, 30% for coloring, with the other 30% for the final adjustments. If the designer has communicated well with the clients in the very beginning, there will be little revision in this stage. Even though some picky clients may still raise suggestions for revisions, there is no need for concern. Because despite these suggestions, they have already approved all the other parts, which means that this project will come to a conclusion in no time. Just take patience and make the final revisions. This process is when the designer is supposed to indulge himself in the sense of success. Make yourself a cup of delicious Mandheling Coffee, and wait patiently for the conclusion while savoring the joy!

The final finish © Perpetual FX Creative

Finish the extended design of the character

3. Ten Key Tips for Character Design

1 Working with a Joyful Mood

It is true that this is your own project, which might mean a lot for you. However, this project should be something you like to do in the first place. If you just want to make a living, you might have taken some easier job. Therefore, it should be remembered that your project is not a demanding task! In addition, what you are looking for is not just the clients' satisfaction. Character design is a creative profession that is highly challenging. Just enjoy the process!

2 Shortcuts to Create Characters

Is there really a shortcut in this profession? The answer is "yes." Don't be surprised. A designer should draw as much as possible. There is no point being obsessed with the finished drafts. Most of them are stairs leading to success. They are not destinations. Therefore, a designer is supposed to put his competence into full play and make bold experiments and exploration in every draft without compromising his usual requirements. A really successful character might just exist in the next draft.

3 Take Every Character Seriously

A designer is supposed to be innovative instead of following conventions. Character design is a creative job. The designer must ensure that his brain operates as fast as a high-speed train. Don't reject innovative ideas in an easy way! You should believe that it is just at your finger tips. Just put down what's in your mind to paper with a drawing pen so that you can show it to others.

Work with a joyful mood

④ The Character Is Real.

We all know that the character to be created does not exist in the real life. However, you should believe that it is real with its own personality, hobbies, friends, families and even pets when working on it. You should give it a life or even a social security number. This character as your creation should be convincing to yourself in the first place in order to survive in others' memory.

⑤ Remember the 3D Property of the Character

Don't take it for granted. This issue has nothing to do with 3D production. What I'm driving at is that when working on any character, the designer should keep in mind the 3D dimensions. Though the character is shown on paper, it is not a card. It is three-dimensional. Maintaining this understanding is important to ensure that the character looks real to the audience, and plays a significant role in the three-view drawings.

⑥ Uniqueness Is a Character's Life

Life is colorful because every person features some unique characteristics which distinguish themselves from others. This rule also applies to the virtual characters we have designed. These characters differ from each other in personality, which means that they will make varied reactions to the same incident and environment. That's what makes the story interesting. The success of any character is determined by how the designer chooses to highlight his unique personality. In other words, uniqueness is a character's life.

⑦ Putting All the Characters Together

It is a good way to test whether the characters are unique enough by putting all the characters together, when you will easily find out whether the audience can distinguish one character from another. Their differences in height, weight, and mood are highly visible when put in comparison with others. Sometimes, even a group of characters wear an identical uniform or take the same joy, they will still exhibit what distinguishes themselves from each other when standing together.

⑧ There Is No Mission Impossible.

A designer never says "no" to his clients. It should be recognized that a designer is only restrained by his own imagination in the virtual world. There is nothing impossible. New characters and new styles are being created all the time.

⑨ Maintaining Curiosity in Everything

Curiosity is very important to a character designer. The character to be created might be a hero living in ancient times, or a warrior from the future. Though it is impossible to be a know-it-all, curiosity will help a designer to obtain a profound understanding of the character and the world it is positioned in so that he can give his character a more convincing and distinctive personality.

⑩ Learning without Holiday

For those who have made up their mind to become a character designer, they are supposed to learn and explore all their life. In this profession which is defined by constant innovation, no one can be successful without continuously updating their styles. Those with a well-developed style might be considered outdated as time goes by. The only solution is constant learning.

A designer should not be intimated by challenges or frustration.

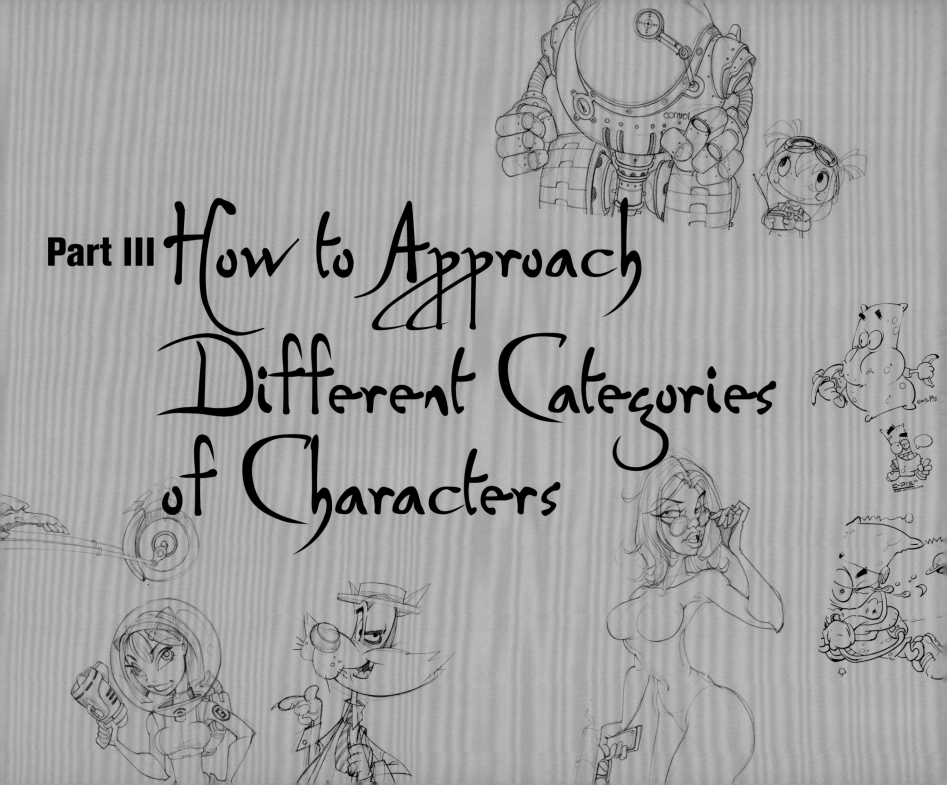

Part III How to Approach
Different Categories
of Characters

This realistic-style illustration is intended as the cover illustration for Germeny's "*Living Art*," a life-oriented magazine concerned with arts. I hope to associate this illustration with some classical-style elements. Therefore, I have selected Titian red as the dominant color which defines Titian's works when coloring the angel with a stretched body instead of using some common colors. Though the picture seems a little striking as a result, the red angel has posed a sharp constrast with the demon crouched in the darkness. This illustration looks amazing on the printed magazine, and has been selected by both "*SPECTRUM 17*" and "*EXPOSE 8*," two top illustration yearbooks in the world. The audience can still identify the meticulous and intertwining lines in the background of this illustration.

1. Female Character Design
— Creating Distinctive Sexuality and Beauty

"What is most challenging is that the designer must strike a balance between common aesthetic conceptions and character's distinctive personality."

The little mermaid

The ultimate objective of female character design is to capture a feminine sexuality and beauty that appeals to human's primitive consciousness. This is a golden rule in female character design. No matter how fashion evolves, female characters who are sexually and aesthetically attractive are always well received.

Beauties featuring distinctive characteristics are always eye-catching in the party, no matter if she is a hot chick or romantic princess, an innocent angel or alluring show girl, a slender maiden or full-figured newly-wed. Our definition of beauty has changed with time. Therefore,

there is no established model to follow which can ensure the character's attractiveness. However, when working on this category of characters, how to highlight their beauty and sexuality should be prioritized as a designer's top concern.

Many experienced character designers still find it difficult to design female characters, because they have to strike a balance between common aesthetic conceptions and the character's distinctive personality. Anyway, female character design is always the most challenging but rewarding part in this creative industry.

1. Preparatory Work for Female Character Design
— Obtaining a Comprehensive Understanding of the Female World

Legend has it that God creates Eve from Adam's rib. However, there is such an evident disparity between men and women in terms of thoughts and behaviors that it is said that the former comes from the Mars while the latter comes from the Venus. This might be the most amazing thing in the world. A character designer is supposed to have a profound knowledge of his character, approach anything without prejudice and be passionate about all the novel and interesting things. A male character designer has to forget his gender and identity when working on female characters to put himself in their shoes. He should be an outstanding stylist, dresser, wardrobe attendant, hairdresser, photographer, and action director at the same time. Patience and observation are of paramount importance for character design. Only by obtaining a comprehensive understanding of the female's life and mental world can a designer get fully prepared for character design in terms of subject, composition, hair style, accessory and color.

"Galactic Fortun" Magazine © Perpetual FX Creative

"Perfect Kitty" Magazine © Perpetual FX Creative

This blonde is a reminder of the late Hollywood star Marilyn Monroe, who impressed the world with her sexuality, passion and blonde hair. I have done a lot of preparations even though it is only a cartoon-style character. I have run through all the literature and photos on Monroe available. The lighting approach and color style in this illustration are both inspired by Monroe's posters, which is intended to produce the nostalgic touch of the pin-up girls by the illustrators of the golden age. © Perpetual FX Creative

VENOMA (selected by *EXOTIQUE 6*)
© Birke & Friends Publishing Ltd

A smoking girl with red hair
art: Haitao Su / color: Dan Wang

2. Physical Features of Females
— Thin Shoulders and Big Butts

Men and women differ in thinking and behavior less than in physical features. However, as women are responsible for carrying and delivering babies, there is still an evident disparity between men and women in physical outline. As shown in the illustration below, this disparity is most visible in shoulders and pelvis. Women are more delicate and smaller than men, and thus their shoulders are thinner and narrower than those of men. However, as for pelvis, women are wider than men. This contrast is more evident in cartoon characters featuring exaggerative styles, which will enhance women's sexual appeal and make men look more agile. Therefore, women look narrower in the upper part and wider in the lower part, with men wider in the upper part and narrower in the lower part. Take a side view of female characters, and we will find a silhouette featuring one reversed triangle on top of another one. There is no doubt that their protruding breasts and hips explain their sexuality.

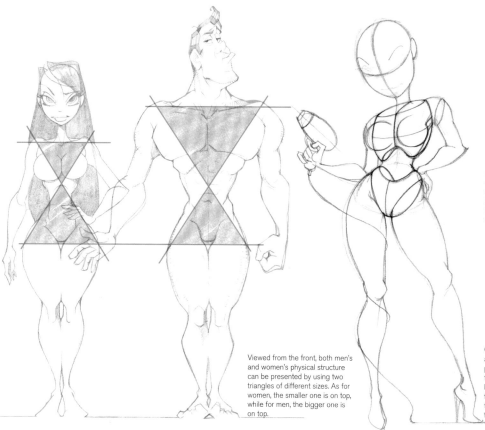

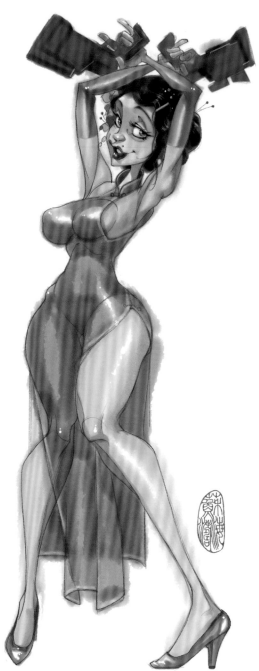

No matter whether it is about Oriental elegance and Occidental charisma, a designer's ultimate pursuit is to use natural and flowing curves to capture the intrinsic beauty and sexuality of women, as shown in the right illustration.

Viewed from the front, both men's and women's physical structure can be presented by using two triangles of different sizes. As for women, the smaller one is on top, while for men, the bigger one is on top.

Generally speaking, it is not easy for a designer to capture these evident physical features. Because in most cases, the human body cannot remain still like lifeless models. A designer is supposed to highlight these features through some flowing and beautiful motions as shown in the left illustration.

Beauties featuring distinctive characteristics are always eye-catching in the party, no matter she is a hot chick or romantic princess, an innocent angel or alluring show girl, a slender maiden or full-figured newly-wed. Our definition of beauty has changed with time. Therefore, there is no established model to follow to ensure the character's attractiveness. However, when working on this category of characters, how to highlight their beauty and sexuality should be prioritized as a designer's top concern.

3. Female Facial Features and Expressions — Note the Proportion and Position of Facial Features

The combination of facial features is of paramount significance for female characters. It might be true that no female can be elegant and sexy at the same time. But it cannot be denied that men's definitions of feminine beauty still have a lot in common. Generally speaking, cartoon-style beauties feature big and round eyes with big pupils, a small and upward-pointing nose (the only facial organ that can be ignored), as well as thin lips glittering with lip gloss. The key to drawing beauties is not to give them beautiful facial features, but to arrange facial features in a proper way. In other words, the proportion and position for different organs are more important than how a single organ looks. My experience is that we can depend on the proportion lines in the drafting stage to adjust the proportion and position. If necessary, the mirror images in the computer can also help to make corresponding corrections.

Show Girl
Face Front+Side View

When working on the front view and the side view, a designer is supposed to keep in mind the sense of space. Horizontal auxiliary lines are effective in ensuring the consistency between different facial features. Any inconsistency between the front view and side view will affect the 3D configuration of the character.

In the right illustration is a set of drafts for facial expressions of Kendra, which I designed for the game "Galactic Bowling." This character is based on the blonde beauty Monroe. In most cases, a designer needs to draw the front view, side view, back view and vertical view of the character, depending on which three model makers can construct the 3D models. The 3/4 view is the most common perspective adopted by the designer, and also the best choice to illustrate a character. Using this perspective can avoid the rigidity caused by perfect symmetry in the front view and the flatness in the side view, as well as help to enhance the sense of depth in a significant way.

All these facial expression drafts are for the blonde beauty Kendra Klein on Page 44.

The design drafts for the black street girl Shanique
Stevens on Page 55

4. Selecting an Appropriate Body Proportion — The Most Common Body-head Ratio is Between Four and Six

Body proportion is one of the basic elements to construct a character. Body ratio ranging from two to nine is constantly used by cartoonists in character design. A body ratio exceeding nine is exclusively applied by fashion designers. Man in real life features a body-head ratio between 7.5 to 8, even though different categories of characters are supposed to feature different proportions.

There is a saying that one can find one thousand Hamlets among one thousand readers. In fact, I have found that every artist has a distinctive understanding of female characters, and usually observes a fixed ratio in drawing characters. Generally speaking, the smaller the ratio is, the more lovely the character looks. On contrary, the larger the ratio is, the more towering and intimidating the character is. Q-style characters featuring a body ratio between two and three will not be covered in this chapter but in the chapter primarily concerned with Q-style characters.

The following drafts illustrate some regular ratios in character design, which might serve as inspiring references for those hoping to draw attractive female characters.

The ratios for characters in the right illustration are common for cartoon characters, which might serve as inspiring references for those hoping to draw attractive female characters.

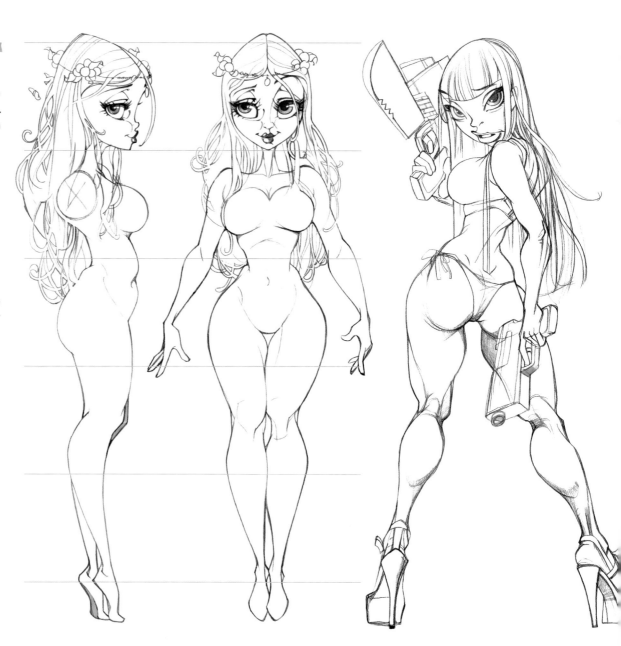

Show Girl
Front View

Show Girl
Face Front+Side View

Vegas SHOW girl
The Vegas theme. 09/7

Design sketches and proportion drafts for
Las Vegas show girls
art: Haitao Su / color: Dan Wang
© Betsoft Gaming

5. Capturing Female Motions
— Dynamic Curves Flowing with Charisma

To capture the dynamic curves is important to illustrate both the character's charisma and personality. Fashionable hairstyle, eye-catching breasts and hips, slender legs and high-heels are all indispensable elements to capture the feminine curves. Some character designers are able to capture the charming curves of females in a flash. Actually, only those with impressive talents and acute observation of details in life can make it in one shot. Like my friend Alberto Ruiz, they have a comprehensive understanding of human anatomy and can highlight the charisma of females with a few simple lines. Daily practice in sketching has helped to enhance their competence in this field. However, to those without astonishing talents like me, they can only depend on intensive trainings in sketching and drafting, observation in daily life and multi-perspective configuration exercises. In the drafts included in this book, readers are likely to identify the following characteristic: the line on one side is nearly straight, while that on the other side is full of curve and rhythm. Such a contrast is visible in illustrations by many character designers, which is an effective way to enhance feminine beauty. I like drafts better than the finish, from which I can identify how they have tried to capture the character's motions.

Heart Hunter

Udon Noodle

This *"Girl with Handgun"* is created based on a photo. Sometimes, creative inspirations will slip away in a flash. A designer is supposed to seize this very moment instead of trying to patch up later.

The kneeling and lying poses of a female character
art: Haitao Su / color: Dan Wang

Halloween Witch,
CG Talk Editorial
Selection Award

Whether the character's poses can convince the audience is determined by the designer's observation of life. The girl with red hood in the draft comes from a scene in my dream. When I woke up in the morning, it suddenly occurred to me that this scene could be transformed into an impressive illustration. I immediately picked up a pencil and put down the remaining illusions in my mind on a nail-size sketch, which finally gave birth to this unconventional illustration.

Shanique Stevens playing the slide board

I have taken many considerations in designing the motions for the black girl Shanique Stevens, including a crotch a little raised on the right, a hand on the waist, and slightly tilted face, which are common poses for adolescents. In this illustration, I have used some typical rebellious gestures to match the trendy clothes, sexy figure, brown skin as well as the eye-catching cassette recorder and bubble gum, which have all contributed to defining the character as a street hooligan.

6. Hair and Costume
— Key Elements to Highlight the Character's Uniqueness and Sexuality

I bet that a designer who is able to manage a rich variety of characters might have problems drawing female characters. I believe that many male character designers share my frustrations — after designing several female characters, we have no idea what other hairstyles and costumes can be assigned to the new characters, because our information on female hairstyle and costumes is extremely limited. An easy solution to this problem is to regularly read female fashion magazines to obtain a considerable knowledge of various hairstyles, costumes and accessories. In addition, I usually ask for some product catalogues when shopping in garment shops and cosmetic counters with my wife, believing that these catalogues will serve as valuable references for me in the future. Of course, a designer troubled with an inadequate knowledge of female materials is advised to choose costumes revealing the back and part of the breasts in order to highlight the characters' sexual appeal.

As for costume and hairstyle, though every category of character is associated with some established stereotype, bold experiments are still likely to produce unexpected results. The beauty in the right illustration wears a camouflage uniform, a typical garment for men, defying convention to define females as gentle and graceful. Thin arms and legs contrast with heavy weapons and boots, highlighting what is special about this character.

A nymph from the fairy tale, whose luxurious costumes refer to Queen Elizabeth's ceremonial robes in the Victorian Era

What is the designer expected to do to demonstrate the nymph's charm in addition to the trendy costumes? The readers can find the answer in the final concept sketch. What I have done with the flowers is just what the clients are looking for.

For most male designers, they might leave out many necessary details by solely depending on their memories when illustrating the costumes and hairstyles of female characters. Therefore, referring to relevant materials will help a lot to construct female characters. The right illustration is based on the role starred by Nicole Kidman in "The Golden Compass".

This is the finish for rival twins in the game "Galactic Bowling." This commission is very challenging. At last, I decided to configure the characters in a cartoonist style (to attract the participation of female players). They have identical faces but oppositional personalities. One is out-going, while the other is always trapped in gloominess; the red one stands for flames, with the other standing for sea. They are actually a combination of harmony and conflict.
© Perpetual FX Creative

Strength and confidence
are what most male
characters are defined by.

2. Male Character Design
— Highlighting the Character's Heroism

> *Illustrating masculine beauty is not about curve or rhythm. Rather, it is concerned with highlighting masculinity through strong lines. Men are always expected to be trusted with important tasks, which determines they have to look serious in the first place.*

Illustrating masculine beauty is not about curve or rhythm. Rather, it is concerned with highlighting masculinity through strong lines. Men are expected to be trusted with important tasks, which has determines that they have to look serious in the first place. A stony face, coupled with wide shoulders, is commonly used to illustrate men of confidence and strength. The swollen muscles underneath their skin are a touchstone for a designer's knowledge of human anatomy. Like in those popular fantasy fictions, we need to give our dream heroes enough strength to lift a huge knife whose handle features ghost motifs or a laser gun with magical power so that he is able to defeat his rivals, or save a beauty from a demon's hands with exaggerative motions — this might be their ultimate mission.

The following passages are intended to explore how to make male characters convincing.

No matter which age the character is set in, no matter how advanced the weapon technology in this age is, bulging muscles are always a signature for heroic males.

1. Basic Physical Features of Men
— A Perfect Combination of Geometric Shapes

No matter in the East or West, no matter in a developed or undeveloped nation, men are always subject to enormous pressure in both society and family. Thus, we have to give male characters a strong stature which can stand the weight of a mountain so that they will not bend in face of any pressure. Wide shoulders are always used to highlight the strength of a male body. The reversed triangle connecting the shoulders and belly button is a reservoir of power from their inner universe. On the other side, men are not responsible for reproduction. Therefore, men's pelvis is relatively narrow in contrast to women to facilitate agility.

The illustrations on this page demonstrate that simple geometric shapes are enough to capture the strength of heroic characters.

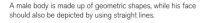

A male body is made up of geometric shapes, while his face should also be depicted by using straight lines.

George B. Bridgmen, the master in artistic anatomy, was a pioneer to use box forms to represent the major masses of the figure, which he referred to as "human anatomy method." This idea seems brilliant even today, because it enables the beginners to grasp the characteristics of human anatomy in a quick way, and makes it easier for the illustrators to draw different gestures in a flexible way, enhancing the liveliness of the character.

In some cases, arrogant characters will appear unnatural. The man in the left illustration is snapping his fingers, which seems a little overreacted.

2. Body Proportion of Male Characters — Properly Exaggerated Proportion

Men's common body-head ratio is 7.5. However, we always expect that men should look a little towering so that they can exude a sense of security. As we can have full control over the characters in the virtual world, more designers tend to use a body-head ratio ranging from eight to nine (which is commonly used in comic books). Therefore, the characters will look powerful enough to survive any disaster and stand the attacks from any intimidating rival. Of course, an overemphasis on body-head ratio might produce a negative effect, because we don't want our character to be someone physically powerful but intellectually incompetent. A body-head ratio at twelve seems to be exclusively adopted by fashion designers.

Though every designer is comfortable with a certain head-body ratio, he will adopt a larger ratio in order to capture masculine power and construct a sense of security when working on male characters. Sometimes, in order to satisfy the audience's obsessions with heroism, the designer will choose to reduce the length of the character's legs to make them more stout. After finishing the front view, side view and back view, the designer has to utilize some horizontal auxiliary lines to help ensure a consistency of height in each body part. Model makers will find it difficult or even impossible to construct 3D models due to inconsistent data unless all the parts on the body or face are identical in every side view.

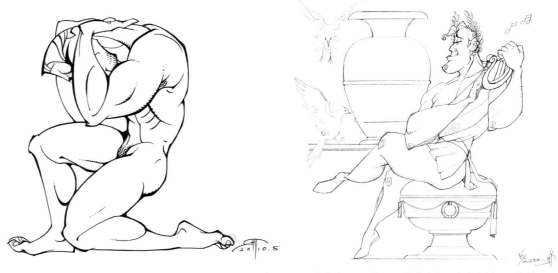

In some cases, the designer can still manage to illustrate men's stout stature and bulging muscles without using gradation and gray scale. The lines themselves are powerfully expressive. The designer can use straight lines to demonstrate masculinity, while making meticulous adjustments of curves to enhance toughness. Of course, this approach actually evolves from typical drawing methods in traditional Chinese paintings.

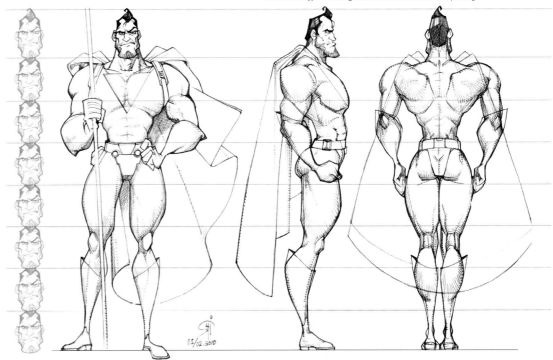

3. Muscles and Skeleton of Male Characters — Anatomy Is the Key

How to illustrate men's bulging muscles and skeleton is a serious challenge to test a designer's knowledge of human anatomy. I will feel amazed if some people can keep in mind the names and positions for every piece of the 206 bones and a number of muscular tissues. Because this is really impressive. Frankly speaking, I'm not one of them, which means that I must have a manual on artistic anatomy at hand. It should be noted that this manual is supposed to be targeted at artists instead of doctors. We are character designers, rather than physicians. We have enough time to examine every part of the body. Such manuals can be found in the arts literature section in the book store. You can totally rely on the classics. The treatise by George B. Bridgmen will serve as good reference for all the artists.

Reviewing works by other artists will also help to enrich your knowledge of anatomy and enhance your interest. Illustrations by Frank Frazetta, Simon Bisley, and Glenn Fabry are the best choices for learners in human anatomy.

Exaggerative muscles and the movements in the corners of his mouth show his arrogance and confidence.

An exercise of super hero

The exaggerative figure has highlighted the
well-trained stature of the swordsman. Male
characters featuring wide shoulders and narrow
waist are commonly found in American-style
cartoons and comics about heroes. But they still
represent an efficient configurative technique.
The only thing to do is to avoid similar gestures
and motions.

A sketch of ancient Egyptian warrior

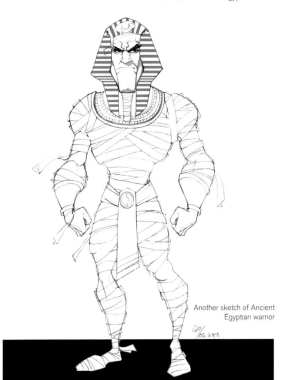

Another sketch of Ancient
Egyptian warrior

4. Gestures and Body Language of Male Characters — Capture the Characteristics of Each Detail

A character designer is supposed to give every character distinctive gestures and body language in accordance with his personality in every drawing except the configuration illustration and the three-view drawings provided for 3D model makers (including the front view, side view and 3/4 view). An outstanding designer should be a good observer in the first place. He can always capture some tiny gestures as defining features of the character. For example, an introverted person will stand with feet pointing inward; someone arrogant is always looking down at others with a lifted chin. Proper body language can add to the character's uniqueness. Even though it cannot substitute knowledge of anatomy, knowing some distinctive features of a certain category of characters will help the designer to decide on the character's body language in a quick way.

Importance of body language is self-evident. No one will doubt it after seeing a series of martial arts movies starring by Bruce Lee.

Bulging muscles are a signature for a physically powerful man Therefore, in drawing male characters, depicting exaggerative muscles is an essential part.

Training in body language is indispensable for stylists. Video tapes for "King of Pop" Michael Jackson is a good reference.

Bravo !

Three versions of "Rocket Man"

5. Costumes of Male Characters
— Creating Distinctive Costumes Matching with the Character

In the last, we have to work as a dresser for our character. No matter if it is the Iron Man's armor, or Super Man's cloak, the costume matches with the character's personality, identity and status in a perfect way. Don't make the audience feel that your character is wearing others' clothes. An outstanding designer will not judge whether a certain design project is successful based on how luxurious the costumes look. These characters are not attending Paris Fashion Week. It should be remembered that the most appropriate is the best. You can have a clear idea how important costumes are in character design through the popularity of COSPLAY performances in comic exhibitions.

An undercover cop during the Prohibition Campaign © Betsoft Gaming

An arrogant-looking casino dealer © Betsoft Gaming

> **Tip**
>
> Character designers are able to express themselves without words, because they can depend on the character's facial expressions, hairstyles, motions, body language, in addition to costume, which is one of the most effective elements to define a character. Costumes are supposed to indicate the character's profession, status, personality, and aesthetic tastes, and demonstrate the designer's personal preferences and styles. Look at the nominees for Academy Award for Best Costume Design, and you can have a good idea what an important role costumes have played in facilitating plot development and character configuration.

An over-confident Special Forces soldier

An athletic construction worker

6. More to Say about Male Character
— What You Don't Know about Men

Men always impress the world with their strength, tolerance, and masculinity. They have been used to hiding their true self in front of others; trying to show only what they want to. Actually, they are also likely to make a mistake. They might be heavy smokers, alcoholics, cowards or liars; they might be possessed with jealousy or addicted to womanizing. A man is a complex of both merits and flaws. No man is perfect. Though there is no point arguing over the complications of human nature, you will find it an interesting task to add some tiny shortcomings to your character, which will help to make him more rounded. It is true! Who can turn his back to a dragon warrior who is destined to save the world because he is greedy about food? Actually, these weaknesses will function to transform the stony-faced heroes into one of us, someone who seems to live in the real world. Just like Chuck Jones, an animation master in our age, remarks, "Comic heroes are not only showing people their heroic deeds, but also their weakness."

Kungfu Boy

Pretension might be a common weakness for men. In order to make this man who likes playing cool before gorgeous ladies to be more attractive, I have spent a lot of effort. At first, I made him hold a match in the corner of mouth. However, in the final finish, I referred to a smoking pose of Brad Pitt, which was also inspired by the initial concept. It does look good!
© Perpetual FX Creative

Escaping from the Jurassic Period
art: Haitao Su / color: Dan Wang

TIP

Using exaggerative perspective effects will help to make the character three-dimensional, more attractive, and more real. No matter if it is one-point perspective, two-point perspective or the more complicated multiple-point perspective, all will work to enhance the sense of depth in the illustration. Application of the exaggerative foreshortening perspective can even help to highlight the character's motions and avoid flatness. In a word, as long as a designer has a comprehensive understanding of principles concerning perspective effects, he will know which is the best perspective for the character or the picture so that the illustration will appear more vivid and interesting.

The character in the illustration seems to be on an adventure in Outer Space or in the Earth's core. Anyway, he looks a little terrified of what is about to happen. Remember to give your hero some insignificant weaknesses, which will make him more vivid and the story more interesting. Do you still remember Popeye, who was a comic star in our childhood? He cannot be more ordinary until eating spinach.

Pinocchio

3. Q-style Character Design
— A Reminder of Our Joyous Childhood

> *What's most special about a character is his facial features, which explains why some designers have chosen to enlarge the head and reduce the body. Q-style characters mostly feature a body-head ratio ranging from two to four, which is similar to that of a newly-born. Therefore, such characters will look surprisingly adorable.*

Actors in the puppet troupe

Many people have heard of "Q-style comics," "Q-style games" or even "Q-style" perfumes. Some might be ignorant of the origin of this term. It is assumed that "Q" stands for "mini," its shape resembling a lovely figure featuring big heads and small bodies. Actually, this term is based on the English word "cute," with which it shares a similar pronunciation. Therefore, people have started to use "Q" to refer to those lovely images. However, the prevalence of this category of characters started from Japan, which boasts of a well-developed comic industry. In the 1970s and 1980s, the Japanese designers began to make derivative products on the basis of popular comic characters. These products mostly feature a lovely body proportion, which later evolves into a new trend in the comic industry. These derivatives include "toy in egg" products, which are called "gashapon" in Japanese.

1. Body Proportion of Q-style Characters
— Learn to Use the Subtraction

A one-year-old baby has a body-head ratio of four. When he grows up, the ratio will increase little by little, normally to 7.5 in adulthood. When working on Q-style characters, designers are supposed to spend a lot of efforts in body proportion in order to highlight the lovely nature of the character. Actually, this is the most evident difference between comic characters and real people. In order to transform real people into cute characters, the designer will go through a process of "subtraction." This does not means that he has to reduce every part to an identical ratio. Actually, this process involves well-calculated selections to keep or exaggerate some parts of evident features, and reduce or delete other parts without any defining characteristics. Through this subtracting process, the character will have all that a Q-style character needs. The most recognizable parts of a character are basically concentrated in the facial features. Therefore, the designer will choose to enlarge the head to adopt a body-head ratio which the newly-born are typical of in order to make the character as lovable as possible.

These characters from the illustrated book "*Journey to the West*" feature a body ratio between 2.5 and 5, as this book is targeted at the children who are not old enough to go to school. Such a design concept can help to bring the characters in the book closer to the readers, by approaching the time-honored legend from a child's perspective.

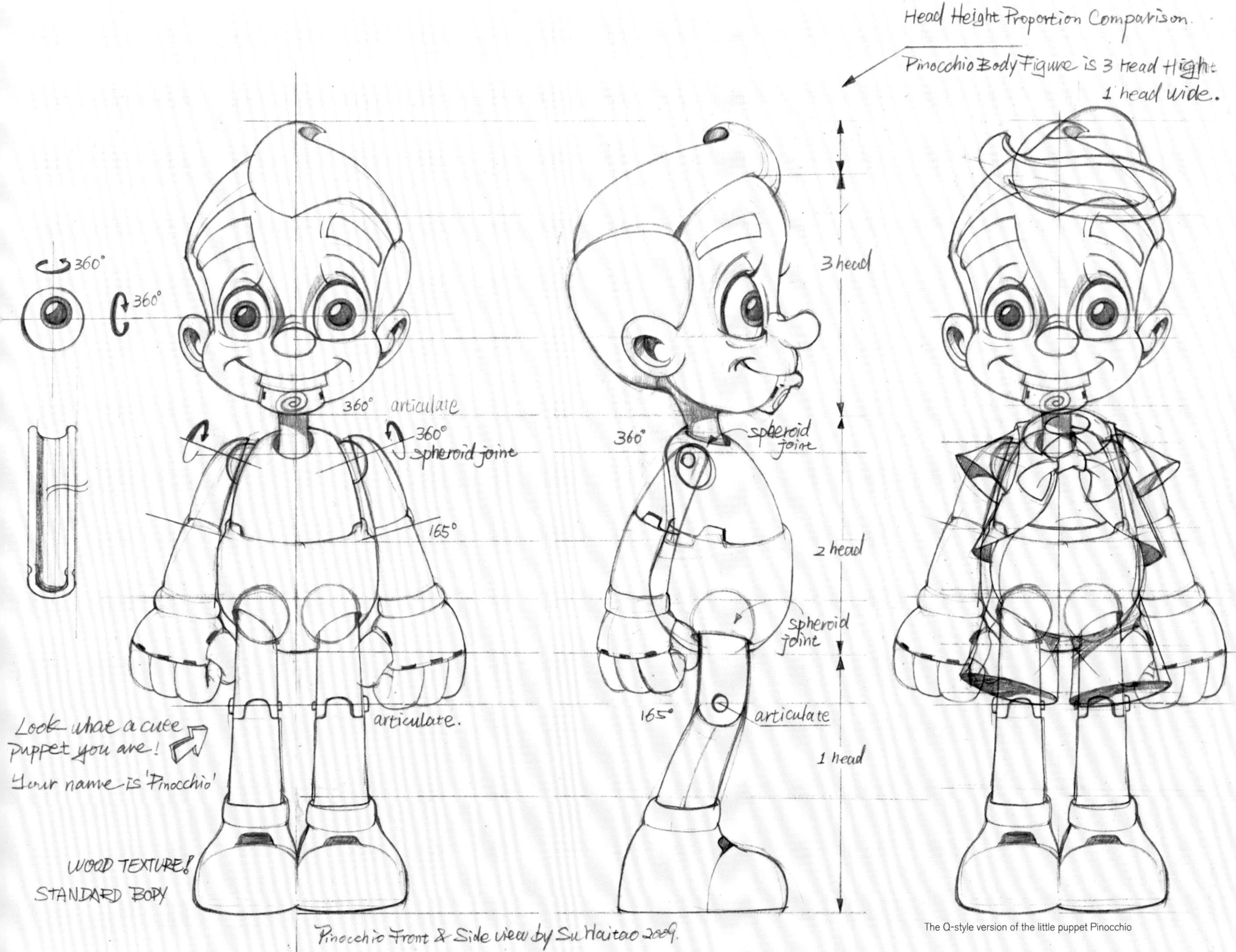

Pinocchio Body Figure is 3 Head Hight 1 head wide.

360°

360°

360° articulate
360° spheroid joint

165°

3 head

2 head

1 head

360°

spheroid joint

spheroid joint

165°   articulate

articulate.

Look what a cute puppet you are!
Your name is 'Pinocchio'

WOOD TEXTURE!
STANDARD BODY

Pinocchio Front & Side view by Su Haitao 2009.

The Q-style version of the little puppet Pinocchio

2. Facial Features of Q-style Characters
— Subtraction Is Still the Key

When working on the faces of Q-style characters, the designer is still supposed to stick to the "subtraction" approach. Eyes are always compared to a window to the soul. Therefore, Q-style characters will always have big and sparkling eyes. The eyebrows cannot express the emotions in an independent way. However, coupled with big eyes, they still play an important role in indicating what the character is thinking or feeling. The mouth is also one of the essential elements to capture various facial expressions as an important "emoticon" for Q-style characters. Ears are not as significant as the aforementioned organs. However, they can also work to give expression to the illustrators' personal styles. In addition to the facial features, the designer can also depend on some distinctive comic symbols to produce a rich variety of facial expressions. For example, the short lines on the character' face stand for the flush on the character's face.

It is shown in the illustration that there is an evident disparity between Eastern and Western Q-style characters even though they belong to the same category.

The process to draw Pinocchio's facial features

The lovely little puppet Pinocchio

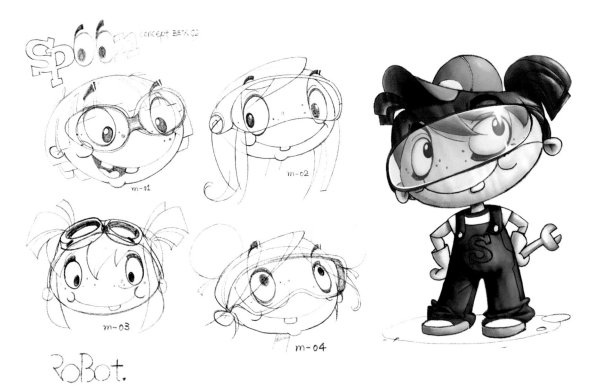

SP66 concept BETA 02

m-01

m-02

m-03

m-04

This lovely girl is a quick-witted hero in one of the iPhone games. The illustration in the right lower corner is the proposal the clients finally selected.

RoBot.

main character concept BETA 02.

m-06.

main CHARACTER ncept BETA 02.

The main character
front view

The main character
side view

The process to design Q-style versions of Tang Monk, Pigsy and Sandy

Eye's

眼窝凹处
盆待后期眼神的填 眼窝放出层底。

眼窝

乙重
眼角

瞳孔

侧面

The Little Match girl
CHARACTER DESIGN.

Little Girl

Goodbye! Pinocchio!

09/11/12

In Andersen's fairy tale "*The Little Match Girl*," the designer has left enough room to illustrate the eyes, which are the most emotionally provocative part. As a result, the nose and mouth have been reduced to a small size. Even though the designer has simplified the face to the maximum extent, the character still features distinctive characteristics. It should be noted that the eyes are positioned in the lower half of the head, which makes the character more adorable.

3. Motions of Q-style Characters
— Keep It Simple

Generally speaking, due to their short stature, Q-style characters cannot complete complicated actions. Therefore, there are some established signature actions for this category of characters. In other words, Q-style characters are always exhibiting the final poses as a result of a certain movement, in contrast to a rich variety of gestures featuring other categories of characters. Sometimes, such poses are too stereotyped and seem a little unnatural. However, the designer can also take it as an advantage, considering that he can capture the unique features of the character with the simplest pose and motion. What is a designer supposed to do if a Q-style character has to perform a certain action? It is advised to leave aside the original body proportion, and reduce the head in order to enable the character to complete a complicated movement. However, it should be remembered that the adjustment should be limited and temporary. Never enlarge the body without considering the original proportion.

TiP

The minimum body-head ratio that can be accepted in character design is two, which means that the body and head have the same height. Such characters are often used in commercial campaigns. Even when the overall height is small (when it's used on a webpage), the designer is still able to put a rich variety of exaggerative expressions on its face. However, there are indeed some disadvantages concerning the Q-style characters. Due to their tiny hands and feet, some complicated poses are too much for them. Remember not to make them cradle their heads in arms, or take any actions involving putting the hands on head or over head. Therefore, this category of characters is not good for story-telling. If it is intended to narrate a story, it is advised to adopt a body-head ratio exceeding four.

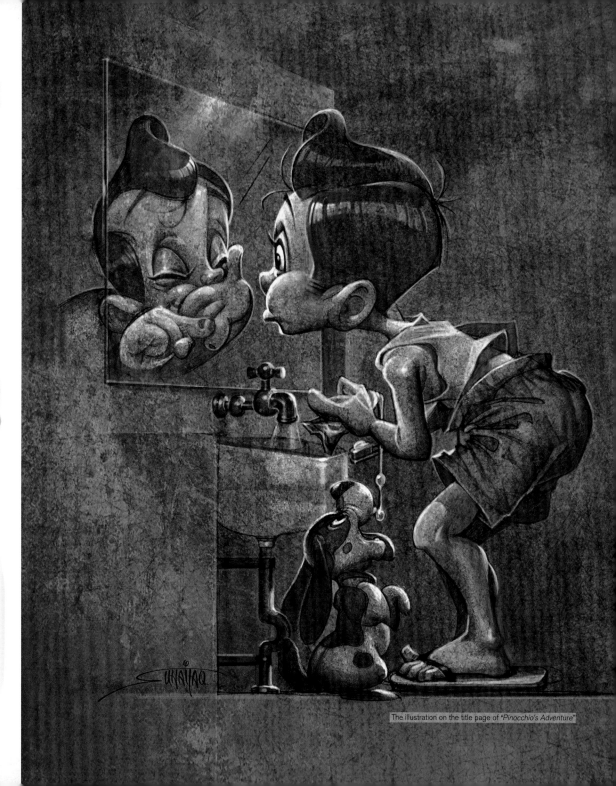

The illustration on the title page of *"Pinocchio's Adventure"*

The puppet is still lifeless.

Another design sketch for the hoodwinked

A girl

A girl

The main character-04

I didn't eat the ice cream!
art: Haitao Su / color: Dan Wang

Just no interest!

A nymph from the fairy tale

Jack and the Beanstalk

Evil Mummy Prince

4. Application of Q-style Characters
— Commercial Mascots Are Loved by All

Due to their lovable nature, Q-style characters are targeted at pre-school students, pupils and girls, no matter in the game or comic industry. For example, games such as "*Kartrider*" and "*Q-style Journey to the West*" are all intended to attract these specific groups of consumers. In recent years, Q-style characters seem to be more appealing to adults. They are commonly used in derivative comic products such as "toy in egg," resin kit, and key chains. In fact, this category of characters is the best option for commercial campaigns as mascots. The merits are very evident. Q-style characters can manage to impress people from any region or speaking any language. They look lovely, honest, and innocent, which is irresistible for people of different ages. They will never grow up or become aged, which is something impossible for stars in real life. All these have explained for the lasting popularity of Q-style characters in the commercial domain.

The character in the cover illustration is inspired by a photo of a dog robber from French Land Force.

Cartoon characters on the package for racer toys

KILL BILL

Exercise for Q-style characters – *"Kill Bill"*
art: Haitao Su / color: Dan Wang

A boy with burning passions

"Hoodwinked" from an animation textbook

The illustration from children's reading *"Journey to the West"*

A Mother's Half Hour

The pirate captain's secrets

Creative sketch

The little mermaid

The flute player

This one-eyed giant is one of my favorites, with an enormous stature and unparalleled strength. However, he is intellectually challenged, no more clever than a five-year-old child.
© Perpetual FX Creative

4. Monster Character Design

— What's Common among These Weird Beings

> *This kind of fictional character is not solely based on broad imagination. They cannot be convincing unless the designer has a comprehensive knowledge of biology.*

A green giant loving pink bunnies

Monster characters are the most interesting category in character design. When working on such characters, the designer can unleash his imagination and experiment with all the possibilities to make the characters as weird as possible. An impressive monster character can bring in fantasy elements to the work and produce some unexpected results by creating suspense and enhancing the atmosphere for the overall story. However, it is not easy for a concept designer to create convincing monster characters. In the following passages, the readers will have a clear understanding that such monsters are not solely based on broad imagination. A designer without adequate knowledge of biology will only end up with characters that are strange but not convincing. However, if a designer's imagination totally gives way to scientific theories, it is impossible to create impressive and unique characters.

1. The Foundation to Create New Species — Biological Principles

A good observer will easily find out that any monster character is not merely a product of imagination, but based on certain creatures that we are familiar with. Studies on known species can help to lay a solid foundation for creating virtual characters. Look at those well-known monsters. No matter if it is an octopus with strangling tentacles, or an alien as a bag of bones, there is no doubt that it has evolved from one or more known species. The monster must have some unique powers which enable it to be a survivor in any vicious environment so that it will not look like the product of sloppy imitation. Even the aliens coming from other planets are not totally inspired by the designer's imagination.

In most cases, we will adopt one of the following three approaches or all the three when working on monster characters.

A Adding some other features to the mutated human or other species;

B Incorporating the characteristics of another one or more species with human or a certain animal to produce a new species or a sub-race;

C Creating a new species by combining the features of several species.

To produce an established formula for character design discourages creative spirit. However, this scientific generalization does provide certain biological guidelines for the character designers. Generally speaking, monster characters based on these principles will turn out to be surprisingly impressive and strikingly convincing.

From the biological perspective, dinosaurs are not supposed to be categorized as monsters, because they did exist on this planet. However, they often star in monster movies. The game character in the illustration is inspired by both dinosaurs and gladiators.

GB
WARP PLANET CREATURE
A space worm, possibly Earthworm Jim type of character with arms and legs.

GALACTIC BOWLING

The front view and side view of worms from the Mars

It was great fun to work on this character. Obviously, it shares a similar appearance with the earthworm on our planet: its slippery and freezing skin might provoke repulsion, which also indicates that it is an inhuman creature from outer space. The audience might start wondering whether its ability to regenerate the lost segments is as powerful as that of its counterpart on the Earth.

© Perpetual FX Creative

2. Biological Features of Monster Characters
— Based on the Close Relationship between the Species and Its Living Environment

ABOMINABLE SNOWMAN

The snowman

Now we have seen some basic approaches to designing monster characters. However, some known species are better choices for "monsterization," while others are not. What common features does the former category share? Sheer size and ferocious nature are not the only criteria. Some creatures, though small and harmless, might seem so threatening and intimidating when reconfigured in an exaggerative way that we might start to worry whether we might fall prey to them. Some creatures always appear in highlight in Hollywood blockbusters, such as the dinosaur, octopus, snake or python, whale or shark, ape, monkey, bat, scorpion, toxic spider, and earthworm. All these creatures feature something lethal or terrifying. Though some of them are small in size, they are more horror-striking than predators such as lions and tigers when taking a larger body. The equations that follow make it clear how to produce new species and their corresponding nature. When working on new species, this "plus" thinking approach is highly inspiring.

Deep sea + Octopus = Abysmal Cannibal
Jungle + Barbarian = Jungle Phantom
Swamp + Snake = Killer Anaconda
Desert + Earthworm = Sand Worms
Snow Mountain + Ape = Yeti (Snowman)
Sky + Pterosaur = Flame Dragon

Spider + Human

Soldier Crab + Human

Boar + Carrion

This is another example of aggressive and ferocious characters. Biologically speaking, it also presents a variation on the ape, like Peter Jackson's King Kong. I have chosen to implant some mechanical components under its flesh to give it a touch of the postmodern punk style.

Unlike Q-style characters, monster characters cannot impress the audience only by being cute, because they are not cute in any sense. What's unique about this category of characters is that they can be threateningly destructive. If the audience starts to be concerned about what will happen to other characters at a single sight of the monster you created, it is certain to be a huge success.

Even fictional monsters are not solely based on imagination. This horrible desert monster has ragged teeth and a big mouth, which are a typical feature of predators. Its earthworm-like body moves in a swift way, while its lethal upper arm is based on the poisonous sting of the desert scorpion.
© Perpetual FX Creative

A beauty in a fierce battle with the bug from the Outer Space

TiP

Though we are only talking about character design, the living environments of these monsters should also be one of our considerations. The jungle, swamp, deep sea, desert, and snow-mountain are typical settings in Hollywood adventure films, where the monsters commonly inhabit. All these locations share something in common. They are all some mystic territories which are unknown or inaccessible to mankind. Humans mostly live on the expansive plain. There's nothing we don't know about it. Therefore, it is not a legitimate habitat for monsters that are usually shrouded in mysteries. A monster living on the plains will be of no help to a mystery or fantasy story in any way.

Desert
Monster

3. Biological Details of Monsters
— Highlighting the Unique Features of New Species

Character design involves more than construction of typical living environment and species selection based on biological principles. The character designer still needs to take consideration of many details. We need to give the monster some trivial biological features that are consistent with the living environments and biological principles concerned, such as the texture and color of its fur, the characteristics of its ears and teeth, how many claws it has and whether it has sharp nails. When working on monster characters, the designer is supposed to ask himself the following questions. For example, considering its living environment, should the monster stand on its hind legs or walk on all fours? Taking account of the temperature of its habitat, should it have fur all over its body, or just over certain parts? What niche does it occupy in the food chain? How do its body proportion and limb length affect how fast it reacts to a crisis? Does it prey on people? Does it have sharp fangs or big molar teeth? Does it attack for the purpose of surviving or taking revenge? Asking theses question will help to make these virtual monsters more convincing, because the process of concept development also observes a scientific approach. If you want to design a predator but make it walk on hoofs, it will still look like a plant-eater, rather than man-eater.

This fierce-looking monster is actually a kung fu master. Though it looks like a lizard, this character is inspired by Kevin Eastman's Ninja Turtles. What I did was to just assemble Michelangelo's upper arm with that of Donatello, and try to make the assembly as natural as possible.

Dino Times
DINO EXPO

www.horshamtoday.co.uk   Friday, March 17, 2006   Telephone: 01403 751200

A dinosaur or half dinosaur half man or a radiation evolved
dinosaur type of creature

DINOSAURGUIDE

DIE GRÖSSTEN FLEISCHFRESSER

Allan Aikins, chief executive of Beales, outside the former Allders site. Photo: STEVE COBB. C6110057

Lost Planet Creature !

Dino Times
COMMENT

ÜBERSICHT (DINOSAURIER)
Camarasaurus
Bedeutung des Namens: Gekammertes Reptil
Periode: Oberer Jura
Hauptgruppe: Sauropoda
Länge: 18 Meter
Gewicht: 15 – 20 Tonnen
Nahrung: Pflanzen
Fossilfundstätten: In den USA
(Colorado, Utah, Wyoming, New Mexico),
wahrscheinlich in Portugal.

Your letters – write to: The Editor, County
Times, 14-16 Market Square, Horsham,
West Sussex RH12 1HD
FAX: 01403 751248
e-mail: gary.shipton@sussexnewspapers.co.uk

In addition to the trivial biological features, depiction of other details can also help to make the works more enticing. Dainty clothes, glittering emerald ring, burning Havana cigar with smokes coiling up his fingers, his stinky mouth, all the details have indicated that he is a vulgar hooligan under the guise of a well-off entrepreneur. It is hoped that readers tend to believe that his bulging purse is full of money earned by trafficking liquor during the Great Depression.
© Perpetual FX Creative

This little game which involves hammering turkeys in Outer Space is actually a bonus from a game package. Though this game is set in Outer Space, the turkey still looks stupid and clumsy. It hops around on one leg, inspired by the crane which seems one-legged in sleep because it has curled up the other one. I have attached some eggs to its neck, because some fish also keep their eggs in the mouth in order to protect them from enemies' attacks. When working on monster characters, the designer often integrates the biological features of some known species and his own creative ideas so that the creature created will seem convincing and real.
© Perpetual FX Creative

This combination of snowman and Sasquatch is a
sensitive trouble-maker, which frequently makes
presence in fantasy and adventure stories.
© Perpetual FX Creative

The savage from the LAVA Planet

4. Infusing Uniqueness into the Monster
— Making the New Species More Vivid

Even the monsters and aliens have independent thinking and distinctive personalities. Sometimes, human beings tend to make hasty conclusions based on the appearance, which might explain why they are always fearful of the "strange" or "weird." Therefore, many monsters are depicted as fierce-looking, which is consistent with the common assumption. They are also illustrated as bloodthirsty, which also exploits the conventional thinking. There is nothing wrong with these characters. It's just that they cannot surprise the audience. On the contrary, if a giant monster is in fact a coward, or a monster preying on man faints at the sight of blood, the designer has succeeded in infusing more vitality into the characters. In addition, such concepts can make the story more interesting by highlighting the character's conflicting personality.

The movie "*Creature from the Black Lagoon*" is one of the classics. The director has successfully convinced the audience that the prehistoric Gill-man is also an affectionate creature who has finally captured the girlfriend of an expedition team member out of love.

"Would you marry me?" A monster character will not look real with human hands or feet. Only when the designer has given it some typical properties of human beings (such as womanizing) can the characters look vivid and lively in a real sense.

Reading stories to monsters

Ogre Monster which is intended to make people laugh

The whale monster in "*The Adventures of Pinocchio*"

5. Mysteries about the Aliens
— Top Secrets

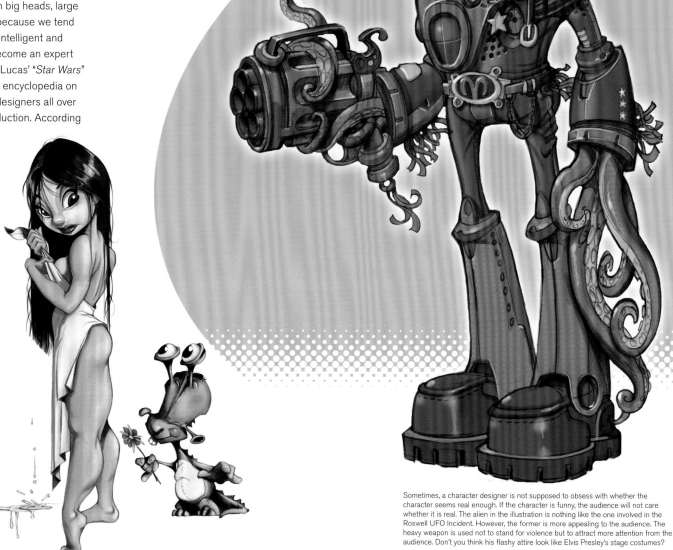

Aliens are making more active presence in more and more fantasy movies and comics. Nowadays, many people would like to image aliens with big heads, large eyes, short limbs but nimble fingers, because we tend to believe that these aliens are more intelligent and agile than ourselves. If you want to become an expert on aliens, it is advised to see George Lucas' "*Star Wars*" Series, which can be enshrined as an encyclopedia on aliens. Almost all the best character designers all over the world have participated in its production. According to my personal experience, it is not difficult to come up with a horrifying alien character. However, to create one with distinctive personalities and sensitive emotions who will never fade in the audience's memory is rather challenging. This might explain the enduring popularity of the "*Aliens*" Series.

Is it playing courtship now? The aliens also love beauties. This little, shy alien differs from the alien monster on Page 98 not only in stature. The most important thing is that the designers have given them different personalities. The smaller one looks more lovable in comparison.
art: Haitao Su / color: Dan Wang

Sometimes, a character designer is not supposed to obsess with whether the character seems real enough. If the character is funny, the audience will not care whether it is real. The alien in the illustration is nothing like the one involved in the Roswell UFO Incident. However, the former is more appealing to the audience. The heavy weapon is used not to stand for violence but to attract more attention from the audience. Don't you think his flashy attire look like Elvis Presley's stage costumes?

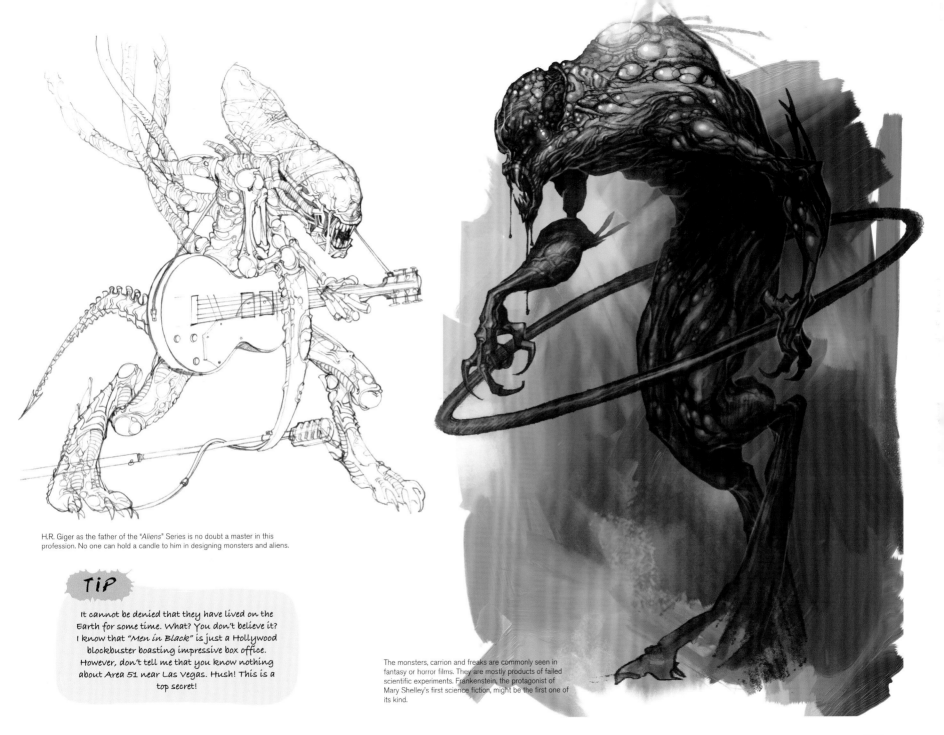

H.R. Giger as the father of the "*Aliens*" Series is no doubt a master in this profession. No one can hold a candle to him in designing monsters and aliens.

The monsters, carrion and freaks are commonly seen in fantasy or horror films. They are mostly products of failed scientific experiments. Frankenstein, the protagonist of Mary Shelley's first science fiction, might be the first one of its kind.

Monstrosity usually brings destructive power.

5. Animal Character Design

— Outstanding Animal Characters Should Be Real in the First Place

> *The best animal character designers are supposed to have a comprehensive knowledge of animal anatomy no matter whether he intends to emphasize its wild nature or adopt a more anthropomorphic approach.*

Dare-to-die Wildcat Soldier

Animal characters are an indispensable category for comics and animated films. It is difficult to imagine what the cartoon industry would look like without animal characters. It must be extremely monotonous and boring! In character design, animal instincts and propensities are still visible, despite an intimate relationship between animals and humans. In the cartoon world, animals can talk, and have independent thinking and distinctive personalities. They share something in common with humans in a certain sense, which can help to make the story or film more interesting and enticing. A considerable number of films have taken full advantage of the humanlike features of the animals. Some of them such as "*Space Slam*" and "*Who Framed Roger Rabbit*" even star both real people and animal characters, which has brought great pleasure to the audience.

1. How to Configure Animal Characters — Should They Be Untamed or Humanlike?

When working on an animal character, a designer has to make a choice in the first place. He must decide whether to personify his character, or let it keep all its "animal nature." There is no established formula concerning how to strike a balance. Actually, the designer has to take good considerations of what the story is about, where and when the character lives, and who this story is targeted at when making the choice. Don't make hasty decisions at this stage, because your decision will concern a number of intricate details. For example, should your character walk on all fours or stand on his hind legs? Should it wear just a vest, or be decently dressed? All these considerations will determine whether your character will make a success. If the animal's nature is prioritized, it will function to highlight the greatness of nature and the primitive instincts of the animals. "*GON*" by the Japanese manga artist Tanaka Masash is representative of this category. Without any dialogue or narration, this manga has marveled the readers with charismatic nature. If a personification approach is adopted, it will help to make the animal characters more interesting and real, which would consequently leave more possibilities for the development of the storyline. "*Tom and Jerry*" is an American animated film which simply centered upon a never-ending rivalry between a cat and a mouse. However, the battles and chases between them have inspired an animated series. Without the ingredients of human personalities, the mouse and the cat would not have made such a big success.

When working on animal characters, a designer is supposed to take accounts of what the animal was born with and what people generally think of it. If there is a certain inconsistency between the former and the latter, the audience might start to raise doubts whether the character is convincing enough. This shark character to intended to make people laugh. Therefore, it is illustrated as a gangster in the real sense. With the tattoos on its upper arm and the toothpick between his lips, he looks like a real rascal. What is most challenging is how to give it arms and legs, which a normal shark does not have as a marine creature.
© Perpetual FX Creative

FUNNY FROG FRONT VIEW

FUNNY FROG SIDE VIEW

A frog that looks like an ordinary frog v.s.
a frog which stands up like human
© Betsoft Gaming

SINGIN' IN THE RAIN

Though there is no audience, the frog named Gene Kelly is putting
on a show in the rain. This illustration is inspired by the classic
Singing in the Rain.

2. The Foundation to Create Animal Characters — Starting from the Animals' Original Characteristics

An outstanding animal character designer has to obtain a comprehensive knowledge of animal anatomy in the first place; no matter he favors the personification approach or celebrates the innate properties of the animals. Those weighing "animal nature" over "human nature" should find anatomical knowledge more important. Only by capturing the animal anatomy in a precise way can a designer manage to encapsulate its defining features and create an impressive animal character. There is no exception. Even the personified animal characters, though exaggerative, are based on an appropriate anatomical structure. Anatomical knowledge applies to the character's looks as well as its postures and motions. There is a rich variety of animals. However, there is no need to study each of them in particular. When studying anatomy, a beginner is advised to start with the animals belonging to the same category. Take the felines which we are relatively familiar with as example. Though cats and leopards differ in size, they walk, run and jump in an identical way.

This hippo is inspired by a real picture. The personification effect has been highlighted with the hat which seems ill-fitting at the first sight.

TiP

Our understanding of various animals is mainly based on TV programs such as "Animal World," "Animal Planet," "National Geographic," and "Discovery." As to BBC's "Walking with Dinosaurs" and "Walking with Beasts," we have to buy DVDs and run through them again and again, which will help us a lot when we are working on illustrations on dinosaurs. Besides, visiting museums and zoos can enable the designer to access relevant knowledge in an immediate way. If you like to put down what you have seen in the sketch book, you can acquire a large amount of firsthand materials in such places. With a basic knowledge of anatomy, the designer is unlikely to make any stupid mistakes, such as being confused about how ostriches and human run.

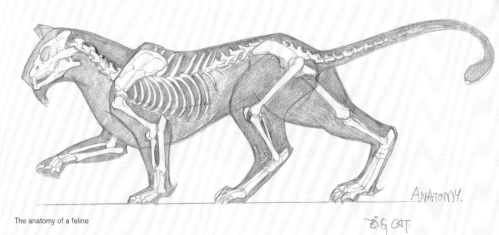

ANATOMY.

BIG CAT.

The anatomy of a feline

A wolf warrior

This running horse features many cartoon ingredients. However, its motions still observe that of real horses.

Wow! Monster is coming...

Good morning, Mr. Dinosaur!
art: Haitao Su / color: Dan Wang

This illustration has highlighted the corn and powerful forearm.

3. Personified Animal Character and Its Motions — Following Your Heart

Personification of animal characters involves a lot of challenges. Firstly, the designer is more or less subject to some anatomical and biological limitations. In addition, he has to take more considerations when elaborating on the details. For example, an animal which is supposed to walk on all fours in the real life might stand on its hind legs so that its forelegs can be freed to imitate human motions, while as for a personified bird, its wings will act like hands. The designer can transform its features into fingers, which was just what the director did in the classic animation "*The King and the Mockingbird*." When working on insects, the designer might find it difficult to deal with its extra tentacles. While elaborating on these details, the designer might exploit the innate properties of the animal in real life. Master Oogway in "*Kung Fu Panda*" exemplified this approach. However, there is also exception to this common practice. The designer might give his animal character a certain feature which will make it totally different from its counterpart in the real world. For example, in the Tarzan Series, there is an elephant who thinks himself a dog; in "*Ice Age: the Meltdown,*" a mammoth firmly believes that she is an opossum. This absurdity has made the story more interesting and engaging. Therefore, don't be restrained by your drawing techniques or the established styles. Listening to the voice of your heart is the most important thing about character design.

A shark gangster

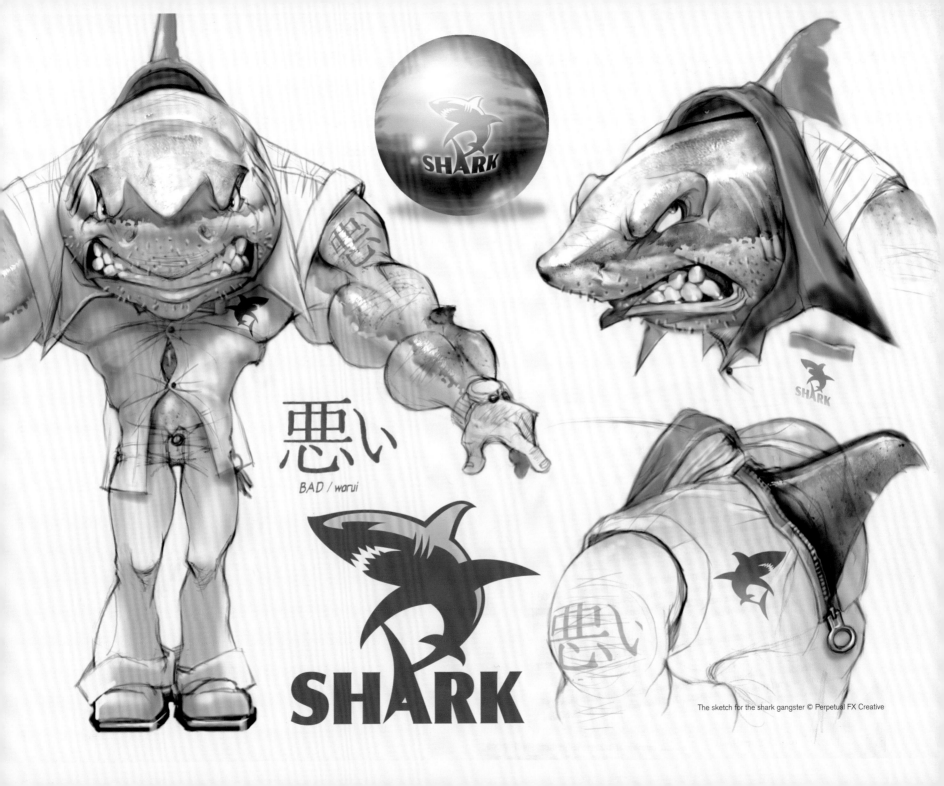

悪い
BAD / warui

SHARK

The sketch for the shark gangster © Perpetual FX Creative

This frog travels a lot. His outfits are quite different from those of the travel lovers at our age, and are based on the ancient attire of the Tang Monk on his pilgrimage to the West to retrieve the Buddhist sutras, though one can find a number of contemporary accessories.

Three Little Pigs

The initial draft for the three pigs

Sherlock Holmes Mouse

The illustration on the right is concerned with the well-known liars who are already eye-catching in Carl Collodi's original, the blind cat and the crippled fox, who have faked their disability. In this illustration, they have been reinterpreted as ridiculous losers who can deceive nobody but themselves. Creased hats, sloppy wind coats, smeary gloves, buttons hanging by a thread, cigarette ends, ragged teeth, and the haunting flies all help to highlight this theme.

Zombie Panda

Kung Fu Panda

Yahoo...!

Crazy Panda

Chef

Knight Panda

Little bear

"Humph!"

Pigwalker

pigwalker.
2010/02/07

Boss Panda

Naughty Mouse

A Girl Riding Dodo. The Dodo went extinct long ago in 1681. They could not fly in the sky like other birds, because their wings already retrogressed. Therefore, they seemed stupid and dull, like something that stepped straight out of the comic books.

4. Different Statures of Animals
— Cute v.s. Big-boned

Animal characters can be categorized into the small-sized, medium-sized and big-sized. In this book, we will make thorough explanations concerning how to deal with the cute-style and big-boned in particular, both of which are very common in character design.

A The cute-style does not only include small-sized animals such as cats and dogs, but also the babies of big-sized animals, such as baby elephants and bears. Like cute-style human characters which we have covered in the earlier chapters, cute-style animal characters are also able to generate affection on the part of the audience. A designer has to observe the same rule when working on this category. It is always taken for granted that such cute-style animals are just miniatures of the adults. Actually, though the former shares some similarities with the latter in terms of anatomy, there is still some difference: unlike the adults, baby animals feature a fluffy

and plump body, large head, big face, short bridge of nose, ragged teeth, nearly-invisible neck as well as padded feet and hairy ears, with big eyes and small mouth placed in the lower part of the face. All these are typical features for this category of animals. Proper exaggeration and application of these special elements will help to come up with eye-catching and well-received cute characters.

B Big-boned animal characters are mostly based on animals featuring big statures and ferocious disposition. A designer can depend on reasonable exaggeration to give prominence to their prowess as well as primitive and untamed nature. Bulging muscles and inexhaustible strength are their lethal weapons. However, overemphasis on their vigor might produce monsters instead of big-sized animal characters. When working on this category, a designer can draw upon typical principles for masculine character design.

Ruthless-looking Pig Detective of Scotland Yard

Three Little Pigs character design

Three little pigs and the bad wolf

Sketch for the Elder Piggy and the Younger Piggy

Piggy as McDonald's deliveryman

Don't look at me!

Piggy in junior class of kindergarden

Piggy brushing teeth

Mr. Phony Wolf

Four different design sketches for the lovely penguin mascot "Mambo"

5. Details of Skin and Fur
— How to Capture the Unique Features of Animal Characters

Though the highlight of animal characters is neither fur nor skin, it is still necessary to have a considerable understanding of how to deal with these details. It is known that most mammals or birds are furred or feathered all over. Then do we need to consider these details when working on character design? To make our characters more interesting, it is advised to attach a clump of fur and feathers to some fluffy parts such as the tail and bird's wing. It should be noted that there is some difference when dealing with cute animals and big-sized beasts: as for the former, their fur will take a rounded silhouette, while as for big-sized beasts, especially those starring bad guys, theirs will project a ragged outline in order to highlight their ferocity and wickedness. In most cases, the designers will observe this principle. There are some exceptions such as crocodile, frog and zebra, whose hide or scale is ridden with certain motifs and patterns. The designer can turn to the suggestive approach when working on them.

Cat

Owl

Spoiled Miss Cat

Mr. Owl

Big Mouth Crocodile © Modern Music Field

"Big Mouth Crocodile" is the mascot for "Modern Music Field," a magazine on pop music which boasts the largest circulation in China. This is the most influential and longest-lived among all the commercial mascots I have designed.
© Modern Music Field

The color finish for the elf © Betsoft Gaming

6. Supportive Role Design
— Make Them Stupid and Ridiculous

Pinocchio's father Geppetto

> " *Generally speaking, supportive roles can never found themselves in highlight like leading roles. However, they are indispensable for the development of the story.* "

on't slight these characters in any way. They stand for the majority who can never make leading characters in the story. However, an animation or story will be incomplete without them. As small potatoes in life, no matter how hard they try, no matter how strong they look, they can never make a success. Just like green leaves crowning the red petals, their ultimate mission is to give prominence to the greatness of the heroes. Positive adjectives such as brilliant, gorgeous and courageous sound alien to them, who are defined instead by ordinary, lazy, careless, stupid and gluttonous, etc. However, they are of enormous importance to the story. Our heroes are always entrusted with important missions. They must keep themselves prepared at any minute to start off to rescue the Earth. Therefore, they have to put on a stony face to play cool from time to time, too occupied to think about how to make the stories more enticing or interesting. Therefore, the supportive roles have to rise to the occasion instead. Sometimes, their ridiculous deeds can trigger intensive responses from the audience, perhaps because we can identify ourselves in these insignificant characters.

1. Supportive Roles — The Importance of "Inconsistency"

There is always something dramatic but weird about supportive roles: a bag of bones with a protruding oval-shaped small head and arched back, reminding the audience of the question mark, or a swelling stomach which does not match with the small head. No matter what they look like, the key is that they can never be gorgeous or pleasing to the eye. Otherwise, they will fail what is expected of them. In the end, the designer has to give them big feet and hands (or small hands and feet to the big-boned), which will make them look extremely stupid.

In fact, when working on character design, I will base on the silhouette of the characters to determine whether they are what I want. Following this method, it is not necessary to finish all the details. Instead, the designer can try to use simple geometric shapes such as a triangle, a circle, oval or square to construct a desired silhouette for the character until all the exaggerative and contrasting elements he wants can be found in the simply-crafted silhouette. At this stage, he can go further to add the details such as facial features, accessories and costumes. This approach has proved to be highly time-saving and efficient to design characters featuring unique characteristics.

Though "exaggeration" and "contrast" are not new, they do work. It is easy to figure out how these approaches take effect through the draft. A towering body threatens to crash the tiny motorcycle. Though it is only a simple draft, the dramatic effects are strikingly evident.

Character designers must take caution to avoid elusive silhouette. In other words, it is a golden rule that the character's limbs should be arranged in different positions instead of overlapping with each other, such as one leg placed before the other one. Therefore, we can base on the silhouettes of the characters to conclude whether they are vivid enough. In this illustration, a tall and slender character contrasts with the other one who is short and fat. This approach shares some similarities with the puppet shows, and is the most simple, immediate and efficient way to produce dramatic effects by depending on visual elements.

Inconsistent body language is a defining and common feature for this category of characters. In this illustration, the man is a little hunched as it is really difficult to support the super huge head with the slim body. However, he still raises two fingers to exhibit his confidence. Though he has tried his best on everything, he can never make his dreams come true (does he remind you of Mr. Bean)?

2. Facial Expressions of Supportive Roles — Eternal Silly Smiles

According to the findings of visual experiments, people will direct their attention to where people show up, and focus on their facial expressions. Therefore, brilliant character designers will try to depend on facial expressions to convey what he wants to say to the audience. generally speaking, facial expressions of the supportive roles are always more impressive than those of the leading roles, featuring listless and half-closed eyes, drooping lower eyelids, and a sleepy face, or big but lazy eyes with no sparkle, coupled with a mouth of buck teeth. Their faces are always ridden with silly smiles as if they care about nothing. Even the approaching catastrophe seems to have nothing to do with him, not because they are positive-thinking but because they are slow in reaction just like prehistoric animals.

"Hi!"

The boss of the puppet circus

A cowboy

A performance man

A pirate

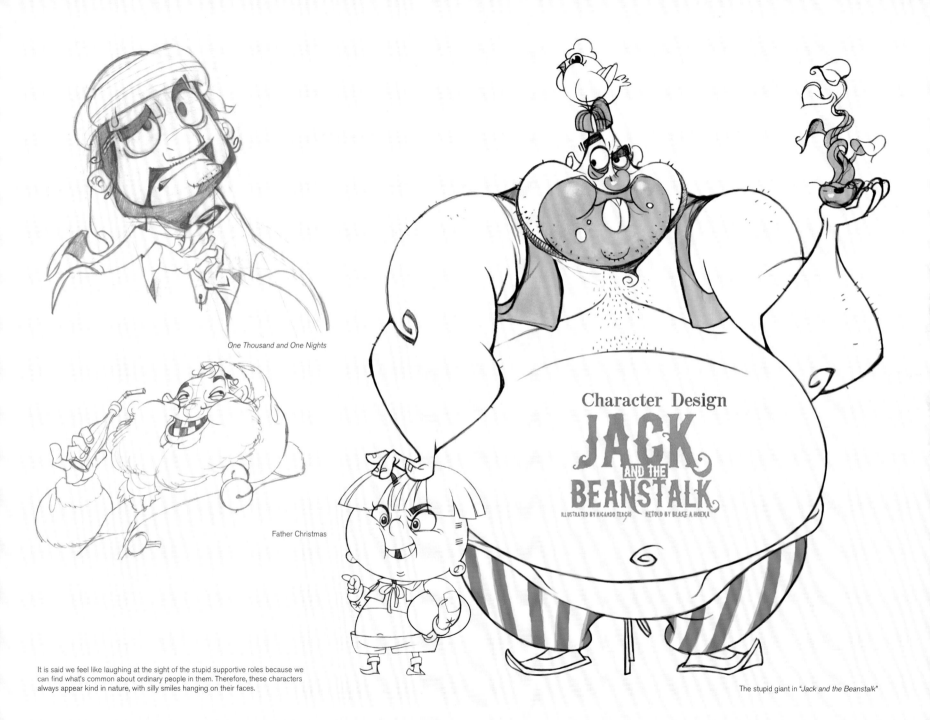

One Thousand and One Nights

Father Christmas

Character Design

JACK
AND THE
BEANSTALK

ILLUSTRATED BY RICARDO TERCIO   RETOLD BY BLAKE A HOENA

It is said we feel like laughing at the sight of the stupid supportive roles because we can find what's common about ordinary people in them. Therefore, these characters always appear kind in nature, with silly smiles hanging on their faces.

The stupid giant in *"Jack and the Beanstalk"*

3. Motions of Supportive Roles —He Is a Comedian

The personalities of the characters can be conveyed through facial expressions and look, while their motions can also work as effective complements. People with different personalities will react in different ways to the same conditions. Their responsive motions will exhibit an evident difference, which is the best way to demonstrate their personalities. People admire Chaplin mainly because he had successfully established a signature style — a gentleman tramp, through his outstanding gestures and motions. Like their looks,

the motions of the supportive characters will seem inconsistent in some ways: hands, feet and body will act at their own will instead of listening to orders of the brain. It is unnecessary to rack our brains to figure out the reasons for this inconsistency. In most cases, these characters will act in different ways from ordinary people at the stimulation of external information, which is why they seem so funny. Like competent actors, the characters in the comic world are also responsible for exhibiting the conceived personalities through their gestures.

All the band members seem carried away by their own music. Do they appear a little ridiculous to the audience? When working on such a small group of supportive roles, it is important to create a difference in silhouette so as to produce a striking effect through this contrast and variety.

Huge M. Hefner

Mr. White Collar

A gentleman tramp

The Pirate King

4. Background Environment for Supportive Roles — Creating Enough Dramatic Elements

We can depend on various approaches when working on supportive characters. Sometimes, you will still feel dissatisfied even though you have used all the aforementioned methods. This is OK. We can also depend on more creative concepts to enrich the character, by designing a simple scene or some necessary props for it. As long as the concept is good enough, your character will look real and vivid. An outstanding character designer will always succeed in making the audience laugh with simple scene props and some auxiliary elements, such as the characters' footsteps, the shadows cast on the ground, a pet or a basketball. For example, he will make a stout man pet a Chihuahua no bigger than a mouse, or make a lovable girl dragged ahead by a roaring and threatening bull dog, which will easily produce a sense of humor through sharp contrasts.

The exaggerative gestures of this character are really funny. However, if the firecrackers, matches and the flames on his hips are removed, we will find it difficult to figure out what the man is doing.

AMAZING!
COMING TO TOWN
THE
SMALL PUPPETS
BIG
CIRCUS

POSTER DESIGN BY CASPER

A poster for the Puppet Circus

AFTER THE SHOW IS OVER, THE BOSS OF THE THEATER GIVES FIVE GOLD COINS TO HIM AS REWARD.

Pinocchio

The circus boss in "*Pinocchio's Adventure*"

5. Importance of the Supportive Roles — Stupid Guys Fight Back

Though the contributions of stupid characters are seldom fully recognized, they are still indispensable, facilitating the transition and development of the story. They cannot only function to highlight how smart and powerful the leading heroic characters are, but also serve as another thread to string up the plots into a complete story. Of course, the dominant thread is still based on how the leading roles fight with the villains. However, the battle between justice and wickedness is too cliché to be eye-catching. Therefore, the designer can only depend on the other thread to bring a new life to the old story. In some stories, these supportive roles even successfully steal the thunder of the leading roles and become the highlight of the story, well-received by the audience in an unexpected way.

The front view and side view of the drummer © Betsoft Gaming

A drummer of a band

TiP

The great illustrator Norman Rockwell once said, "I think those who are thirsty for others' attention are just the ordinary characters in the ordinary scenes." Inspired by this theory, all his characters radiate a sense of familiarity and humor. We have always spent enormous efforts on the heroic characters. However, they only exist in fiction and film. It is those ordinary and stupid characters with some evident flaws that come out of real life, that are worth studying and exploring.

Butler
classic butler
in a tux. He
serves drinks to
Mr. Vegas.

Butler
classic butler
in a tux. He
serves drinks to
Mr. Vegas.

Sorcerer © Betsoft Gaming

9. Bad Guys

— How to Make Them Evilly Charming

> *A designer can challenge the conventions at his will when working on villains, trying every means to make them unique and special. They are always cooking up some amazingly intelligent conspiracy, wicked but charismatic.*

EGYPTIAN EVIL MUMMIE

A vicious mummy

There is always something interesting about villains, in every sense. This category of characters crystallizes the designer's creative concepts. The rise and fall in the story determine whether the story is interesting and convincing. Therefore, how these bad guys perform is a primary premise for the success of the story. These villains are professional trouble-makers. In contrast, the heroes can only react in a passive way. There is no exception. The good guys are good in a uniform way: they are supposed to be honest, benevolent, courageous, and warm-hearted, which means that there is nothing special to make them stand out from each other. However, as for the villains, we can ignore the conventions, making them look bad in different ways. We can give them some super clever crime schemes, defining them as wicked but charismatic. The more clever they are in committing crimes and making trouble, the more interesting the whole story will sound. Therefore, in some sense, these bad guys are the real driving force to facilitate the development of the story.

1. Draw Villains
— Straight Lines and Closed Angle

Most villains share something in common in terms of their looks, though these common features do not apply to each and every villain. In contrast to the upright heroes that are made up of a round or square structure, villains are mostly constructed on the basis of triangles. Triangles feature sharp angles, which will keep people away for fear of being pierced. Therefore, the designers have exploited this property of triangles to indicate the menacing and treacherous personalities of the bad guys. Thus, the audience can always identify many hidden triangles in this category of characters. We will talk more about designing bad guys in the following passages. However, it should be noted that using straight lines and sharp angles is the most common and efficient way. Since childhood, we have reached the understanding that things with sharp edges or angles might hurt us. Therefore, a character could take advantage of this deeply-rooted assumption to give prominence to the wicked, ferocious and threatening nature of the bad guys.

John Dire

John Dire with a gun

John Dire is a villain endowed with both experience and competence. A silhouette based on straight lines has captured how powerful and awe-inspiring he is. Such a seasoned trouble-maker will be a headache for the leading roles, making the story more interesting and enticing.
© Perpetual FX Creative

The design concept of this clown is inspired by the Joker Clown in "*Batman*," which I loved very much. The toys hanging down from his neck and the untied shoestring all indicate that he is a stupid thief careless about the details.

A waiter who is both wicked and sinister

The aged Dracula. His arched back not only suggests his senior age but also his evil and deceitful nature.

2. Gestures of the Villains
— Distorted Motions

Though looks can roughly define a certain character, a designer is also supposed to depend on gestures for a complementary purpose, just like in a mime. The audience knows what is going on on stage because the actors have used their bodies as props. Sometimes, body language is more powerful than dialogue and facial expressions, because it represents a natural expression of the character's emotions. The gestures of the villains are also determined by their inner emotions. In contrast to the open gestures of heroes, those of the villains tend to be closed, distorted and deformed as a result of their negative sentiments such as jealousy, pessimism, insanity, wickedness, hatred, dismay, frustration and anger. These intense gestures will help to facilitate the development of the story.

Count Dracula. His arched back has been depicted in a more exaggerative way.

The commercial success of "*Resident Evil*" results in an active presence of zombies in games and thrillers. As their looks are generally established, the designers have chosen to spend more efforts on their motions and gestures. Character designers tend to avoid closed and distorted gestures. However, such gestures are the visual elements which need to be highlighted when working on zombies. © Perpetual FX Creative

One of the pencil drafts for the werewolf

Devil Satan. Protruding tusks and bent horns suggest his sovereignty over the dark world, and his evil nature.

3. Facial Expressions of Villains
— Capturing Their Wickedness through Details

It takes considerable experience to capture the facial expressions of the bad guys. They are different from the ordinary people in a subtle way when it comes to frowns and smiles. Their wicked and snaky nature are evident in the corners of their mouth and the tips of their eyebrows. Even though they are smiling in a complacent way, they are supposed to burst into a hysterical laughter or hideous smiles. Due to its psychological disequilibrium, this category of characters always attempts to hide what they truly feel in a painstaking way. However, their attempts always proved to be too lame to be natural. Therefore, even when smiles are still lingering in the corners of their mouth, their eyes are still sparkling with guile and greed. In some cases, they will radiate with an intoxicating sense of mystery, while in other cases, they will be possessed by hysteria.

An expression draft for John Dire

TYPE **1**

TYPE **2**

TYPE **3**

TYPE **4**

TYPE **5**

TYPE **6**

Every character designer has a distinctive habit. When working on bad guys, I tend to draw one eyebrow higher than the other, which will make them more vicious and treacherous, discontented with everything in the world. This approach will help to capture their distorted inner world, and impress the audience in a more profound way. The sketches for Dracula's facial expressions exemplify this point.

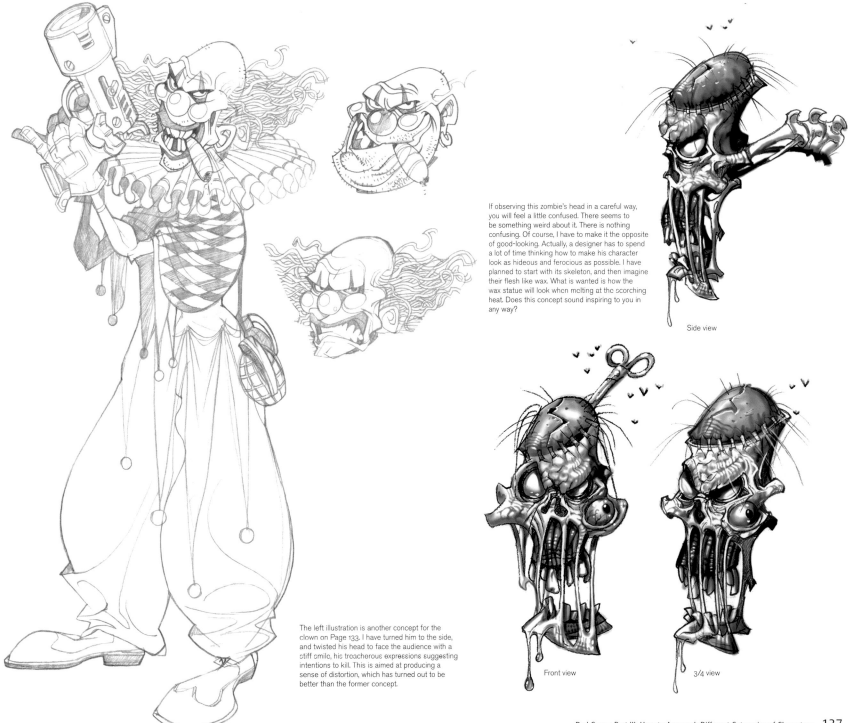

If observing this zombie's head in a careful way, you will feel a little confused. There seems to be something weird about it. There is nothing confusing. Of course, I have to make it the opposite of good-looking. Actually, a designer has to spend a lot of time thinking how to make his character look as hideous and ferocious as possible. I have planned to start with its skeleton, and then imagine their flesh like wax. What is wanted is how the wax statue will look when melting at the scorching heat. Does this concept sound inspiring to you in any way?

Side view

The left illustration is another concept for the clown on Page 133. I have turned him to the side, and twisted his head to face the audience with a stiff smile, his treacherous expressions suggesting intentions to kill. This is aimed at producing a sense of distortion, which has turned out to be better than the former concept.

Front view

3/4 view

4. Light and Shade of Villains
— Unconventional Lighting Effects

The lighting effects play an important role in enhancing the atmosphere in stage performance. When working on character design, we can also depend on the light and shade effects to distinguish between good guys and bad guys. It should be remembered that heroes always stand in highlight, bathed in normal sidelight or toplight. In contrast, bad guys always try to conceal themselves in dark and moist corners, just like the mice and cockroaches which we loathe. As for these characters, the lighting sources are positioned below or on the side instead. In this way, the character's face will obscure in shade due to inadequate lighting, projecting a blurry outline. In this way, the character is fraught with wickedness and darkness.

In my childhood, I had seen a movie on a werewolf. The movies at that time cannot compete with the contemporary blockbusters in terms of technology and special effects. However, due to a calculated application of light and shade, the pictures in that movie still make me thrill with horror. In this illustration, the dominant lighting is positioned overhead, leaving the eye sockets of the werewolf in darkness, making the green sparkles in his eyes stand out like the wolves in the background. In addition, I have used the magic lighting beam in his left hand to illuminate its side outline. A combined use of dominant lighting and supportive lighting have added to the sense of mystery and complicatedness of this character, which is just what is intended to convey to the audience.

A second draft for the werewolf

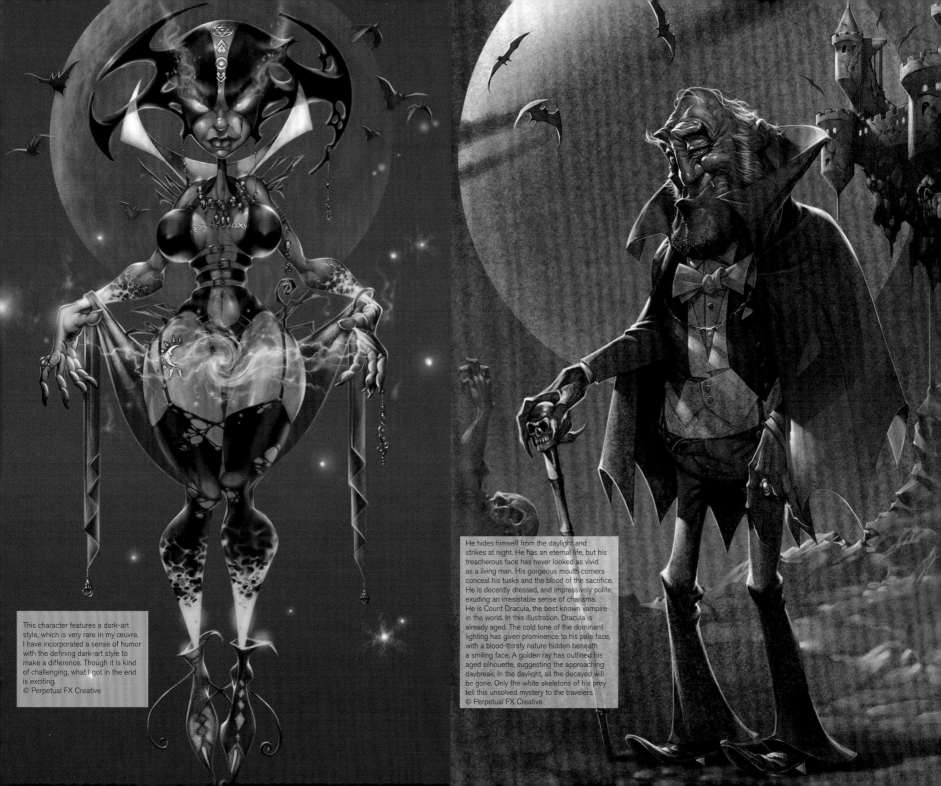

This character features a dark-art style, which is very rare in my œuvre. I have incorporated a sense of humor with the defining dark-art style to make a difference. Though it is kind of challenging, what I got in the end is exciting.
© Perpetual FX Creative

He hides himself from the daylight and strikes at night. He has an eternal life, but his treacherous face has never looked as vivid as a living man. His gorgeous mouth corners conceal his tusks and the blood of the sacrifice. He is decently dressed, and impressively polite, exuding an irresistible sense of charisma. He is Count Dracula, the best known vampire in the world. In this illustration, Dracula is already aged. The cold tone of the dominant lighting has given prominence to his pale face, with a blood-thirsty nature hidden beneath a smiling face. A golden ray has outlined his aged silhouette, suggesting the approaching daybreak. In the daylight, all the decayed will be gone. Only the white skeletons of his prey tell this unsolved mystery to the travelers.
© Perpetual FX Creative

5. Accessories to the Supportive Roles — Masks and Tattoos

We can base on what can be seen in the real life when working on character design. Therefore, we should pay attention to identifying some common features for the antisocialists through newspapers. They smoke heavily, tattoo themselves, wear masks during the robbery, keep their nails long, favor the black clothes (a color associated with death), wear sunglasses and skull-motifed accessories, and have scars on face. Though such items also appear on other categories of characters, they will look like emblems of evil when you find them on the villains. If you still feel that is not enough, you can make the villains pet snakes, lizards, spiders and bats. These fear-striking pets will highlight their wicked nature.

Beneath the gorgeous appearance is a distorted soul without passions or justice.

The outline is made up of straight lines, which indicates how ruthless and indifferent the character is. The shrouding cloth strips give prominence to such properties. The extending bandage is intended to direct the audience's attention to the character at the center of the picture.

rank simbols

Marine simbol
tattoo

dog tags

Details of John Dire's costumes, including his tattoos and
the logo on his T-shirt
© Perpetual FX Creative

"*Vegetable Story*." Inanimate character design involves more than giving the objects eyes and mouth. The designer is supposed to think hard about how to transform what can be commonly found in daily life into something special and vivid. First of all, he should give them a soul which can be easily understood. Therefore, he has to take account of the original properties of these characters. For example, an egg can be configured as a cake baker.

8. Inaminate Character Design
— Creative vs. Recognizable

> *It should be noted that inanimate characters cannot be as agile and elastic in motion as animate beings. They are supposed to retain their original forms in any case.*

Hallomas – the Pumpkin Guardian

What distinguishes this category of characters from others is that they are lifeless objects, such as pencils, cups and lamps. However, in the comic world, all these originally inanimate characters are endowned with life, thoughts, as well as the abilities to communicate and move around. As character designers, we can give them the personalities, habits, language and motions as we like, which is, in my opinion, the most amazing thing about this category of characters. There is no essential difference concerning how to design inanimate characters and other characters. However, it is noteworthy that inanimate characters cannot be bendy and stretchy as animate beings. They will retain their original forms in any case, which poses serious challenges to a character designer. An experienced designer can always strike a balance between flexibility and legitimacy to ensure that his inanimate character has both individuality and vitality.

1. Inspirations for Inanimate Character Design — Gift the Lifeless Objects with the Beauty of Life

This category of characters can be based on a wide range of subjects. All the things around us can be transformed into inanimate characters, such as apple, strawberry, banana, cup, toothbrush, soap, pencil, bag, exercise book….the list goes on forever. All these lifeless daily necessities will make impressive cartoon characters when endowed with a unique personality. The readers might still remember the mechanician master in Akira Toriyama's "*Dr. Slump*" has invented a talking alarm clock with hands and feet. Every morning, it would chant something like "The sun rises up! So hurry to get up!" If Arale has chosen to ignore it, the clock will start to pull her ears. The "Penguin Village" has turned out to be a huge commercial success because all the items that are commonly seen in daily life have been transfor med into cartoon characters so vivid and lively. It is true that in the cartoon world, a designer should not be restrained by painting techniques, or being restricted to certain styles or schools. We can go as far as our imaginations can take us. Now, you will feel eager to pick up your drawing pen and translate something that interests you most in life into an illustration featuring your own style.

"*Napoleon Crossing the Alps.*" When working on inanimate character design, a designer can choose anything as his subject. He will find himself more restrained by his imagination than his techniques.

2. Techniques Concerning Inanimate Character Design — Some Basic Approaches of Personification

A character designer will find it challenging to give life to inanimate characters and produce something what will make the audience feel a warmth rising from the bottom of the heart. This involves more than attaching a face to an object, which is just what an experienced character designer tries to avoid. The following approaches are based on experience, which makes it easier to incorporate the facial organs, feet and hands with the object in an integral way.

Ⓐ Additive Approach:

The additive approach takes three forms. A designer can use the original object as the character's head and / or body.

In the former passages, it has been mentioned that a character designer will avoid simply attaching a face or facial organs to an object. However, this personification approach was widely used in the early years of character design, because it is the least complicated and difficult way to transform a lifeless object into a cartoon character. However, this approach has an evident disadvantage: a designer will end up with something awkward or absurd if he knows little about how to incorporate objects and human elements in an integral and natural way.

Ⓑ Borrowing Approach:

This personification approach involves more challenges than the last one, because the designer is required to find certain parts in the object itself and transform these parts into facial organs or hands and feet in an exaggerative way. Take the car in "Who Framed Roger Rabbit" for example — the headlights are its eyes, with the bumper being its mouth, and wheels its hands and feet. This personification approach has taken good consideration of the object's intrinsic anatomy or composition and transform

Little Pie, the mascot for "Comic Pie Magazine." According to my original concept, this character would be a master of martial arts. However, this character was too short-lived to exhibit all his skills.

TiP

When using additive approach, a designer does not have to add all the elements such as hands, feet, and facial organs to the objects. He can make selections based on what he wants, because inanimate characters are not expected to move and act totally like human. If it can do something that a man does, that's already enough.

The little alarm clock based on the additive approach   The little singer based on the borrowing approach some of its original components into his body parts. However, the question is that how to facilitate a natural transformation. My personal solution is that I would draw some drafts of the pre-transformation objects in my sketch books, and amplify the exaggerative effects little by little. Inspirations will pop out during this progressive process.

Ⓒ Association Approach:

Some products or services are not something we can touch with hand. In such cases, neither the additive approach nor borrowing approach works. Therefore, the designer has to turn to the association approach by using some images that are already known to substitute, suggest or symbolize the original products. For example, we can use lightning to stand for power companies and flames for gas companies to highlight the unique properties of their products. In addition, a designer can also incorporate the initials of the name for the product or the company and its logo as parts of the commerical mascot, or print them on the mascot's costumes or its body to make it easier for the audience to remember the company, enterprise, or product through association.

Ⓓ Hybridization Approach:

In most cases, it will be difficult to strike balance between retaining the evident features of the original objects and producing personification effects. If so, a designer has to incorporate more than one approaches in the creative process, which is called hybridization approach. No matter which approach the designer has used, no matter whether it is complicated or not, the key is that his character has to preserve the intrinsic propoerties of the products, while demonstrating a unique personality and featuring a distinctive style.

Ⓑ Innovation Approach:

With the development of the comic and animation industry, commercial mascots have become more and more popular. In order to esnure the originality of these characters and avoid similarities in style and subject, some enterprises have required character designers to adopt a more innovative way and choose some unknown and unreal things as subjects, such as angels, demons, witches and unicorns, as well as aliens from the Outer Space and big-footed monsters haunting the thick forests, whose uniqueness has made them good choices for commerical mascot design.

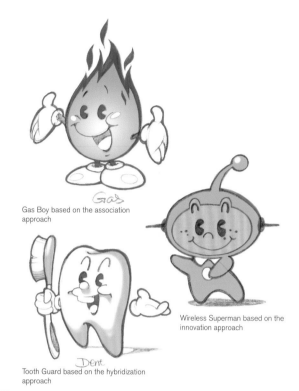

Gas Boy based on the association approach

Wireless Superman based on the innovation approach

Tooth Guard based on the hybridization approach

Category	Characteristics	Advantages	Disadvantages	Examples
Additive Approach	A designer will use the object itself as body while adding hands, feet and head for the sake of personification.	It is the most uncomplicated and immediate way in cartoon character design.	It is difficult to ensure an integral combination of irrelevant objects and human elements.	Little Alarm Clock
Borrowing Approach	A designer is supposed to find certain parts in the object and transform them into facial organs, hands and feet through an exaggerative approach.	A designer can depend on this approach to produce natural and impressive characters featuring a sense of familiarity.	This approach is more challenging than the additive approach.	Little Singer
Association Approach	This approach applies to some products or services that we cannot touch with hand. In this case, the designer has to turn to the association approach by using some images that are already known to substitute, suggest or symbolize the original products.	This approach is intended to impress the audience in a profound way by giving the products or services a concrete image.	Consumers will fail to associate the character with the original products if the designer has made an impropoer choice.	Gas Boy
Hybridization Approach	This creative approach incorporates more than one personification methods.	This approach is intended to exhibit the characteristics of the products in a comprehensive way.	It might cause confusion and misunderstanding.	Tooth Guard
Innovation Approach	A designer will choose something that does not exist in the real world as subject.	A designer can depend on this creative approach to produce characters featuring unique characteristics.	It is difficult to associate the image with the products.	Wireless Superman

3. Exceptions in Inanimate Character — Commercial Mascots

Cartoon characters belong to graphic language that functions independently from verbal expressions, and present an ideal promotional approach for commodities that are targeted at the global market. A considerable proportion of inanimate characters are intended as commercial mascots for certain products and enterprises. Some of them such as the Michelin Man are household names. As a product of personification, a commercial mascots always features a distinctive personality and exudes a sense of familiarity. Therefore, it will leave a deeper impression on the audience than the original product, which is just what the marketing campaigns are aimed at. A designer is supposed to be aware of what approach is used to enhance consumers' impressions on the product and the enterprises. The additive approach involves using the product itself as the mascot, while the borrowing approach is concerned with attaching the initials for the names of the enterprise or the product and its logo to the mascots, such as printing the letters on its costume or body. In addition, some enterprises have depended on the association approach to design their mascots, such as using lightnings to stand for power companies, or flames for gas companies. The Michelin Man mentioned in the passage above is also based on this approach.

In our age, more and more products are competing with each other for the consumers' attention. In this context of firece competition, commercial mascots have played a more and more prominent role in marketing campaigns due to the following merits:

A Highly impressive: commercial mascots features simple but vivid visual images. These mascots are not dependent on verbal expressions, but more eye-catching than letters and logos.

B A sense of familiarity: commercial mascots are primarily intended to bring the product closer to the consumers. The designer is supposed to keep this ultimate objective in mind when working on these mascots. Therefore, despite their age or nationality, all the consumers will find the mascots extremely adorable. In this sense, a commercial mascot is the best spokesman for the product.

C Unchanged properties: commercial mascots are virtual characters based on the designer's imaginations. Differing from the real stars or models, they will stay unchanged — they will not grow old as time goes by, or victimize the sales of the products by causing certain scandals.

D Flexibility: commercial mascots mostly feature a cartoon style. Unlike real stars, how they look on the posters or in the commercials are not subject to the restrictions of photographing conditions. Therefore, they appeal to consumers of different ages, take various sizes, and can reach the audience through different media such as newspapers and TV, compatible with varied promotional approaches.

Sunshine © Sunvision

Cool Bear © Sunvision

Bean © Sunvision

Magic Dream © Movieshow magazine

Little Devine Dragon

9. Mechanical Character Design
— Give the Icy Metal Unique Personalities

> *An outstanding designer is supposed to give a lifeless mechanical character some personalities and sentiments that are exclusive to mankind in the real world. A character has to be unique to be memorable.*

I have defined this category of characters as "mechanical characters" instead of "robots" in order to interpret it from a broad sense. Otherwise, the Tin Woodman who has accompanied Dorothy throughout her adventure in "*The Wonderful Witch of OZ*" has to be excluded from this chapter. The Tin Woodman and his counterparts are based on man's understanding and application of metal materials. They can represent the roughness of the primitive weapons, or crystallize the state-of-art technologies; they can work as a driving force to development of the human society, or turn into cannibals thirsty for man's blood. There is no definite conclusion

concerning whether they are virtuous or vicious. However, we know it for sure that ever since they started to be used as elements or subjects for the sci-fi films, they have been given various sentiments such as happiness, sadness, anger and joy like human beings. There is no doubt that with the development of the film industry, many mechanical characters that we have been familiar with have been outraced in terms of function and appearance. However, the R2-D2 in "*Star Wars*" which looks like a trash can and Astro Boy who has impressive prowess have stood the test of time, without having faded in our memories.

The birth of F-robot
art: Quino / idea: Haitao Su
© Fantasy magazine

1. Anatomy of Mechanical Character — Geometric Forms and Perspective Effects

It has been mentioned in the former passages that a designer should approach this category of characters as if they are people with personalities and sentiments. However, when working on mechanical characters, the anatomy issue is a top concern for the designer. Generally speaking, such characters are built upon a serious of geometric forms. In addition, mechanical character design actually presents a serious test to a designer. Whether a designer can deal with complicated robots is determined by whether he has a profound understanding of perspective effects. In other words, the designer can imagine himself as an industrial designer, whose mission is to finish an industrial or mechanical design. An incorrect perspective effect will directly lead to a mistaken or infeasible mechanical structure.

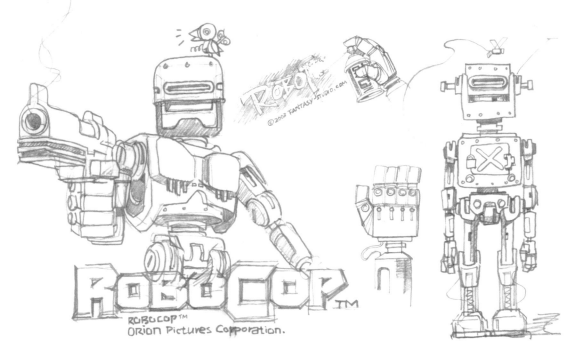

ROBOCOP™
ORION Pictures Corporation.

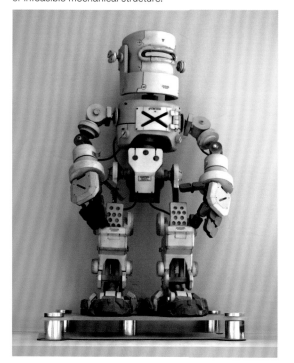

F-robot, the model for the fantasy robot; designed by the author and made by MAMX Model, forty centimeters in height and around 500 grams in weight. He has fifty movable joints. Among them, twelve can move in different directions, while the other thirty-eight can move on the same plane. It took around two months to make this model.
© MAMAX / Fantasy magazine

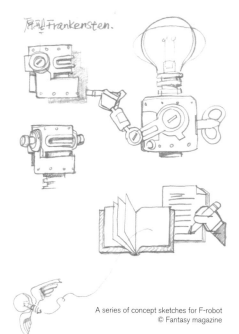

A series of concept sketches for F-robot
© Fantasy magazine

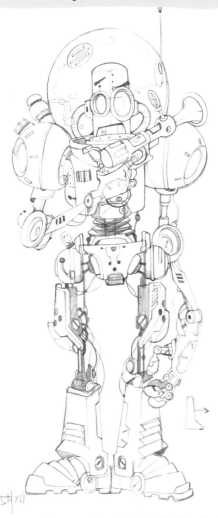

Robot Exploration III (testing version) is produced by the Outer Space Development Administration. It is wondered whether this iron robot with slender arms and legs can survive the harsh conditions in the Outer Space.

2. Sources of Inspirations
— Unharness the Imagination

Unlike robot research institutions, we are discussing about mechanical characters not for the sake of making a breakthrough in the scientific domain. Instead, our concern is how to give these characters some unique features which are originally exclusive to mankind. Human anatomy, facial organs and other body parts are defined by a strict symmetry. A designer can draw upon real people for inspirations, or depend on some occasional incidents or unconsciousness coincidence for enlightenments. In the famous Rorschach Test, the researcher will drop a drip of ink on paper, and fold it in half. Following this, a man will be asked to observe the symmetrical shape, and then tell the researcher what he has seen on the paper. Finally, the research will come up with an assessment of his psychological states based on his answers. When we were young, we were encouraged to lie on the meadow, trying to figure out whether the clouds drifting in air looked like rabbits or bears. Actually, both activities are intended to trigger people's imaginations. Nowadays, the creative process can be finished by depending on the computer softwares. However, the initial concept is still a product exclusively produced by the designer's thinking.

TiP

A designer has to study how the notion of robot has developed in order to construct some successful mechanical characters. "Robot" refers to the mechanical equipment which can operate on its own.. The word "robot" first appeared in "Rossum's Universal Robots" by a Czechic writer called Karel Čapek less a hundred years ago. This fantasy show is about a protagonist called "Robot," who is faithful and hard-working. His name is a combination of "Robota" (literally translated as "labor") and "Robotnik" (literally translated as "worker"). The robot man is a recurring them in literary works. However, should it be considered a man or just a machine? In the domain of character design, we have to define a robot as a she or he instead of it. Talking about robots, we cannot ignore the "Three Laws of Robotics" which was brought forward by the science fiction master Isaac Asimov in 1940. This established theory concerned with the robots' morality and ethics is highly accessible on the Internet, and has posed a profound influence on all the sci-fi works about robots.

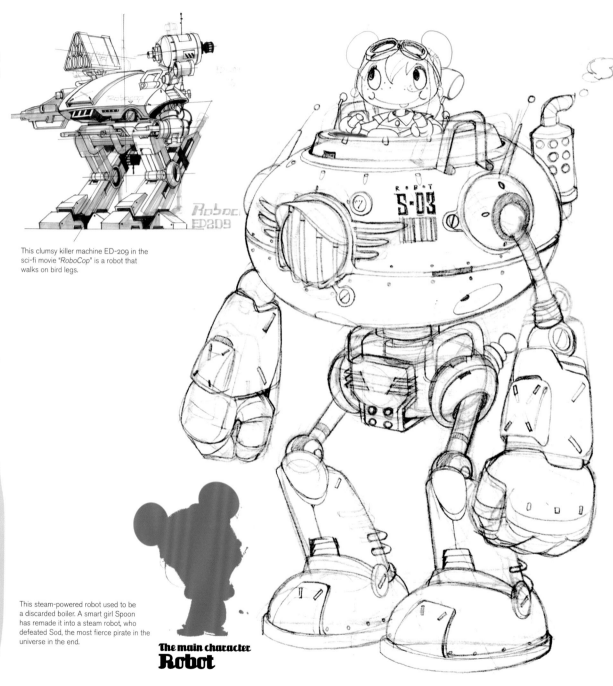

This clumsy killer machine ED-209 in the sci-fi movie "RoboCop" is a robot that walks on bird legs.

This steam-powered robot used to be a discarded boiler. A smart girl Spoon has remade it into a steam robot, who defeated Sod, the most fierce pirate in the universe in the end.

The main character
Robot

The Final Charcter Design.
Spoon

SpoonHero

P.A.L.

P.A.L.

CUATION

The main character
front view

The main character
side view

The front view and side view of the steam-powered robot © Entertainment Work

3. Application of Bionics — Give Life to the Icy Machine

Since their birth, robots are produced to serve the people. The inspirations for this category of characters come from man himself. Robot specialists have to base on bionic theories when working on the look and structure of the robots, while character designers are also supposed to have a profound understanding of some bionic notions. Should your character bend his knees forward like birds or backward like human? Which choice is more suitable?

A designer should take good considerations of the robot's living environments and personalities when making decisions. Besides, an outstanding designer can give a lifeless mechanical character some sentiments that are exclusive to mankind in the real world. The robot can be benevolent and helpful, or hostile to mankind or evil in nature. Anyway, it should be impressive and unforgettable.

Robots are machines in the first place, which are produced to mimic or substitute man. A designer can also draw inspirations from other creatures such as dinosaurs and kangaroos when working on robots, as shown in the illustrations.

This robot is based on apes.

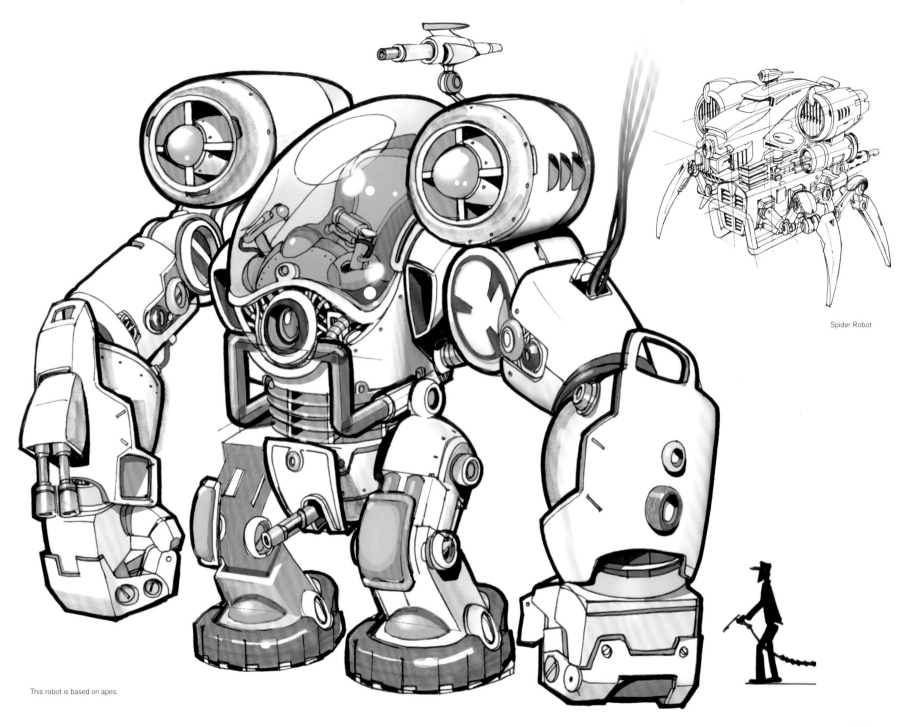

This robot is based on apes.

Spider Robot

4. Add Proper Details
— Give Every Robot Its Unique Personality

A designer has to pay due attention to the details to make his character look real. Robots belonging to varied categories and ages differ from each other in mechanical structure, as well as how their joints move and how the energy transmits. If a designer has made a mistake in the detail, his character will be unconvicing or even a bit silly. According to my personal experience, even a designer might have broken down the hanging clock in his childhood, it is not advised to solely depend on the memory to finish all these details. Instead, he should refer to some photos and materials on machines, especially those depicting the details, inner structure or certain components. In the following passages, I will make a rough categorization of mechanical characters based on how technologically advanced it is. Though this categorization is not scientific enough, it will help those interested in mechanical character design in their learning process.

Ⓐ Tin Man

Exemplified by the Tin Woodman in the "*The Wonderful Witch of OZ*," this category has little to do with technology. In the literary works, a tin man assembled by several pieces of tin can act as someone with thoughts and personalities. In addition, we can give him various sentiments or give it a primitive, or nostalgic touch.

Characteristics: If you are a collector of tin man toys in the 1950s or 1960s, you will draw a lot of inspirations from them. All these toys have crystallized the overall characteristics of this cateogry, which features a simple inner structure hidden beneath a deceiving garment.

Representative: Tin Woodman

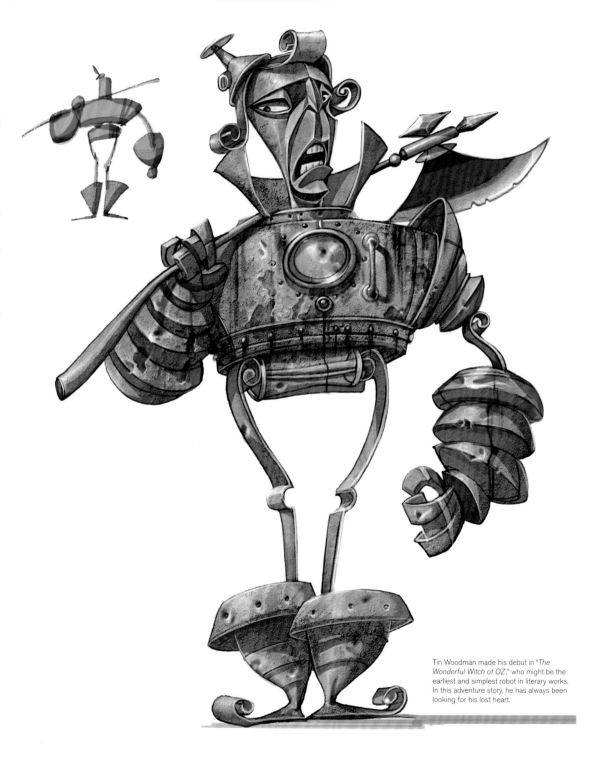

Tin Woodman made his debut in "*The Wonderful Witch of OZ*," who might be the earliest and simplest robot in literary works. In this adventure story, he has always been looking for his lost heart.

B Steam Age

A nostalgic trend has brought us back to the Steam Age, when the seemingly irrelevant words "steam" and "punk" have made up the most fashionable term. "Steampunk" style pays tribute to the nineteenth century, when steam was used as the primary power. Featuring a strong nostalgic touch, this style also celebrates imagination as well as a co-existence of the advanced and the outdated.

Characteristics: A designer can make choices from mechanical components such as propeller, gear and bearing. The seemingly outdated and primitve components actually hold high-technology energy which is powerful enough to make a change to the world.

Representative: Steam-bot

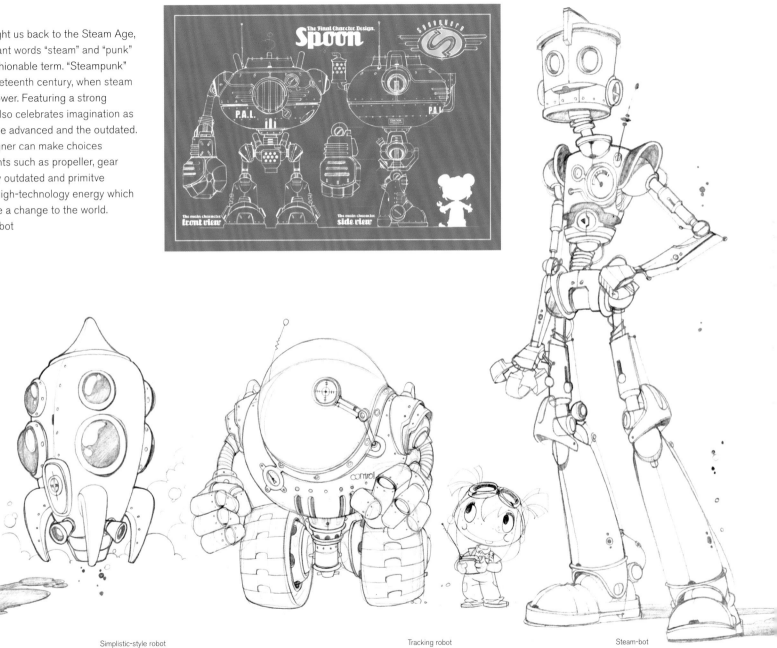

Simplistic-style robot

Tracking robot

Steam-bot

C Intelligent E-bot

Poorly-crafted tin and cumbersome structures are irrelevant to this category of robots, which boast glittering titanium alloy garments and meticulous circuit board. We are currently using robots such as AIBO, ASIMO and QRIO as toys. Maybe they will develop into industrialized household robots some day. Who knows?

Characteristics: as they are intended as household facilities, this category of characters feature slippery surfaces, which exudes a sense of security and reliability. They are more adorable than their counterparts.

Representative: E-bot

The maniac scientist who swears to destroy the world and his big-footed robot

E-bot who is engaged in e-service industry

D A.I. (Artificial Intelligence)

A.I. is short for Artificial Intelligence, and is based on the emulation, extension and expasion of human intelligence. This theory has enabled the original lifeless mechanical characters to make intelligent reactions to the external stimulation or environment through auditory, visual and kinetic experience, making it act in a humanlike way. Astro Boy is representative of this category, and is concerned with a story between machines and people in an age of advanced technology.

Characteristics: due to the technological limitations, we cannot depend on this approach to make robots in real life. However, in order to highlight their humanlike nature, a designer always make them act like common people.

Representative: A.Intelligirl

This Astro Boy is difficult from the original in the book.

A.I. Robot Beauty

As city cleanser, CR800 A.I. Elite Robot is responsible for eliminating illegal trading which has violated "Robot Component Trade and Sales Regulations."

E Bioroid Robot

This category of characters makes frequent presence in the sci-fi films. However, I don't think they belong to mechanical characters in a strict sense, because they are a combination of human bodies and machines. The director Paul Verhoeven produced "*RoboCop*" in 1987, which talks about how a policeman based in Detroit has been transformed into a robot who is proof against gun shots and sword cuts. In my opinion, this character is the most ruthless and humanlike robot.

Characteristics: the stiff and icy alloy components have pierced through the blood and flesh tissues, which is a defining nature for this cateogry of characters.

Representative: RoboCop

The initial draft for bioroid pirate Sod

The second draft for bioroid pirate Sod

The stout diver Dam was attacked by sharks in an accident. He was barely breathing when Dr. Paul came to his rescue and conducted a bioroid transplantation which was still in the stage of experiment. Though his living cells only account for 30% after the operation, these parts have integrated in a perfect way with the liquid alloy injected into his body. In the following years, Dan has fully exploited his astonishing perseverance and incomparable strength and became a well-known hero.

Captain Sod
SPACE PIRATE

Dean Yeagle

Dean Yeagle started his animation career in Philadelphia, where he married Barabra and celebrated the birth of their daughter Becky. Later, Dean moved to New York and worked as designer, animator and director. In 1986, he joined hands with Nancy Beiman and set up Caged Beagle Productions which was focused on serving other animation studios. Their clients include a number of top Amercian or European production companies, such as Walt Disney Productions, Warner Bros, MGM, the Jim Henson Company, Playboy, Blue Sky Studios, Marvel Comics, Hana-Barbara Productions, Random House, and Publishers Group West etc. Dean was named Animator of the Year by the National Cartoonist Society. In addition to animation, he also works on a continuing series of children's books, designs the occasional toy, and contributes cartoons to Playboy magazines. His best-known character is the blonde beauty Mandy with sexy body but innocent nature. In other words, he'll do pretty much whatever swims before his startled gaze.

Please visit http://www.cagedbeagle.com/ to know more about Dean Yeagle.

@ Dean Yeagle

@ Dean Yeagle

@ Dean Yeagle

©2002 Dean Yeagle

© Dean Yeagle

Stephen Silver

Born in London on August 30th in 1972, Stephen Silver started a professional career in 1992. The next year, he set up an illustration company "Silvertoons," which was named after himself. In 1997, he was employed by Warner Bros as a professional character designer for TV animation. He has worked as a Character Designer and Supervisor for Disney Television Animation, Sony's Feature Animation and Nickelodeon Animation. Silver has brought to this world "Kim Possible," "Danny Phantom," and directed the animated series "Clerks" with Kevin Smith. He claimed the esteemed National Caricaturists Networks "Golden Nosey" in 2000, and won National Cartoonists Society's "Television Animation Award" for the design of Disney's "Kim Possible" in 2007. As a successful professional character designer, Silver is also a teacher for online character design courses of www.schoolism.com, and has authored five books on character design.

Please visit http://www.silvertoons.com and http://www.stephensilver. blogspot.com to know more about Stephen Silver.

© Stephen Silver

Gallery * Appendix

Florian Satzinger

Florian Satzinger is a well-known character designer and author based in Austria, and was the student of Ken Southworth, who used to work as the animator and animation director of Disney, MGM and Hana-Barbara Productions and produced many masterpieces such as "*Alice in Wonderland*," "*Woody Woodpecker*," "*Tom and Jerry*," "*The Flintstones*," "*Peanuts*," "*The Smurfs*" and so on. Florian is currently working for S&H FEATURES, and engaged in product design, character design and script writing. Recently, he has been committed to his first comic "*Star Ducks*," while drawing "*Toby Skybuckle*" Series for the French Soleil Productions, and "*Childwood*" Series for a Canadian publisher. He was the concept artist and character designer on many projects for Red Bull, Warner Bros, and Worldwide Publisher. In addition to his designing and production undertakings, he also takes a teaching post in Salzburg University of Applied Sciences, and specializes in character design, simulation and animation history.

Please visit http://www.satzingerhardenberg.com to know more about Florian Satzinger.

© Florian Satzinger

© Florian Satzinger

Francisco Herrera

Born in Mexico's Campeche on December 8th, 1976, Francisco Herrera was employed by Disney's Mexico Commodies Department as a freelancec character designer in 1998. In 2000, Herrera helped produce "*Spyboy & Star Wars Tales*" and was soon accepted by the mainstream comic industry in the United States. From 2001 to 2003, he had cooperated with another Mexican comic genius Humberto Ramos and finished "*KMKZ*" for DC Comics, which was his first solo project. Meantime, he had set up his own studio, which produced "*Thunder Cats*," "*Superman*," and "*Teen Titans Go!*" for DC

Comics in the following years. From 2003 to 2005, he had been working on the "*Spiderman*" Series for the Marvel Comics, and "*Soulfire*" Series for Michael Turner's Aspen Comics. At the beginning of 2008, he was employed by Dream Works as a concept designer, and later moved to Paris to participate in the production of "*The Prodigies*" as a character designer. He had established the RABIA Toys with Humberto Ramos, Jarge Juarez and Leonardo Olea. Currently, Herrera is still working on other animation films for Warner Bros and Anima Studios as a character designer and art director.

Please visit www.herrerabox.com to know more about Francisco Herrera.

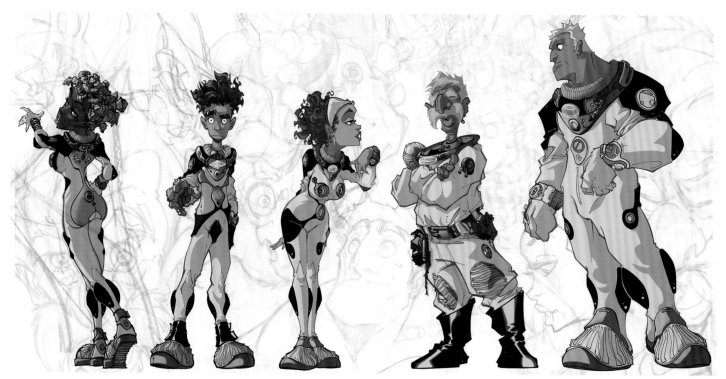

© Francisco Herrera

© Francisco Herrera

© Francisco Herrera

Ben Caldwell

Born in 1973, Ben Caldwell is a graduate of Parsons School of Design for Illustration, and Eugene Lang College for Ancient History. In the last decade, he has been engaged in toy design, animation, children's book illustration, comic illustration and other jobs relevant to arts and design. He was mostly commissioned by Toybiz (a subsidiary of Marvel Comics), and his works include "*The Lord of Rings*," "*Spider-man*," "*X-man*, "*WCW*," "*Harry Potter*" and so on. He also designed the cover for comic books such as "*Justice League*," "*Wonder Woman*," and "*Star Wars: The Clone Wars*." His best-known works are the comic textbook series "Action! Cartooning." In 2005, he was nominated by the Russ Manning Award for Most Promising Newcomer in Cartooning. Currently, Caldwell is working on "*Dracula*," "*the Adventures of Tom Sawyer*," "*World War*," "*The Wonderful Wizard of Oz*," as well as the "*Wonder Woman*" Series for DC Comics. Now, he is living a happy life with his wife, daughter and dog in New York.

Please visit http://www.daredetectives.com and http://purgetheory.blogspot. com to know more about Ben Caldwell.

I Have Taken in the Refreshing Scenery All Along the Road

— An Interview with Haitao Su

Article by Vincent Zhao

During my stay in Harbin, I found myself disturbed by the reckless drivers on the road. Every car seems to be in a rush, striving to outrace each other while avoiding the rotating monitor camera. I was concerned about whether we would arrive at our friend's wedding ceremony on time, when Mr. Su tried to put me at ease: "Don't worry! I'm a fierce driver!"

I had always taken for granted that Su is a peaceful and reposeful man who is never in a hurry. I found myself totally wrong. It surprised me when I saw a multi-functional GPS in his car which can serve as a music player. It was Su's habit to listen to pop music and typically European DJ music. I teased him, "European-style illustrations matching with European-style music?"

"Haha! I don't think the music has anything to do with my works. Actually, I would like to listen to some soothing songs such as those by New Age. I don't know the reason. When seated in the car, I just want some music featuring strong beats, such as the Modern Talking's songs which used to be popular in 1980s. They are awesome! Besides, I will turn up the volume and open the ceiling window. Maybe I'm a little outdated."

China Youth Press has decided to publish this book by Mr. Su. As a coordinator between the two parties, I feel honored to have the opportunity to interview Mr. Su, who has played different roles in my life, from my childhood icon to my supervisor at work and my friend in life. However, he has always been a great influence to me. It is just due to his influence that I have determined to make a person who has an uncompromising insistence on quality and principles, and a lasting passion about my profession, instead of being anxious to achieve success. In the last few years, I have come across his interviews by different media. I want to make a difference this time. I know it for sure that it will be the most important interview in my life, and I hope that this interview will have some influence on the readers.

It seems that we have shuffled between extremity throughout the interview: fierce or reposeful, swift or slow, innovative and traditional, international and local, complicated and simple….the list goes on. The thread to string up these extremities is an artist's instincts to pursue novelty.

"Is it an expression of split personality, just like Dr. Henry Jekyll? A man looks mild and even a little introverted in daily life. However, when holding a drawing pen or steering wheel in hand, he will be a different person."

"Haha! I haven't gone that far! I just like novel things. Anything that I haven't seen before will interest me, especially in drawing. I like to draw things that I seldom see or have the chance to do in real life. Therefore, don't read me wrong! I never smoke, and have no temper-control issues. All my explorations of the unknown world are realized through the drawing activities. Of course, like the majority, I also like beautiful girls, but I'm not a womanizer or playboy. Or it might be said that I have tried what Dr. Henry Jekyll does at night only on my canvas."

"Novelty" was a recurring theme throughout the interview. Passion to explore the unknown realm is a celebrated property for an artist. Mr. Su said, "In 2007, I attended the Frankfurt Book Fair, when I took the chance and visited several European countries. From then on, I have been addicted to the fun of travelling around. No matter my destination is a Chinese place or a foreign state, the local snacks and its history and culture always interest me. Just like I said before, I like new things, and traveling around gives me opportunities to experience the sense of novelty. If I cannot go out traveling, I will channel my passions into painting — embarking upon the journey or adventure on paper."

Talking about traveling experience, I still remember

an interesting incident. I was waiting for my plane with Andrew Jones and another two Chinese artists at the airport. Taking a seat, Andrew took out a notebook and started to sketch, while the other two just idled around. Su once said that some artists in this profession had the habits of "drawing around," which impressed you a lot. However, it seems that a Chinese designer does not share the same habits with his foreign counterpart.

"Wow! You are very frank with what improvements the Chinese designers are supposed to make! It is true that some of the foreign artists will start drawing at any time in any place. It is also true that we Chinese artists don't have that habit. Though I have drawn a lot of characters in my sketch book, most of them are inspired by google photos. When I was young, I could still run into people drawing in their sketch books or behind the erected easle in the park. But that's no longer the case now. Therefore, I start to ask myself whether we are too dependent on the computer. I hope that I myself also have the courage to sketch with strangers passing by. Actually, I have already bought a sketch book. I hope that the next sketcher you run into will be me."

Personally speaking, I think this difference in habits has something to do with the cultural contexts. If we run into someone who is painting in public in a foreign country, we will take it as a beautiful scene. However, in China, we might jump to the conclusion that he is selling paintings for a living or pretending to be an artist. This prejudiced assumption is deeply-rooted among the common people, and has affected the artists to a certain extent, triggering a sense of timidity in their subconsicousness. However, Mr. Su believes that it is just a lame excuse, because no one is holding you back. After all, it is still a personal problem. "I think an artist will earn others' admirations if he is courageous enough to draw in public."

"YOHO!" once staged a national campaign themed on "Worshiping the Trendy." One of my friends implored me to recommend someone based in Harbin. Though Mr. Su seems to have nothing to do with "trendy," I still asked my friend to visit Su's studio, promising that he will

find what he is looking for there. The following interview had turned out to be a great fun. Though the two of them are different in background and age, my friend was still excited when he was back. He was most impressed by the bookshelf in Mr. Su's office, believing that it was really cool to have a shelf full of books in this digital age.

"Actually, buying books has developed into a hobby or habit. It is primarily aimed at taking in novel things, not only concerning the drawing techniques, but also the ideas — the concept. This seems more important. Reading books is like befriending with someone or taking a trip. I don't have many friends, and I don't have much time for traveling around. Therefore, I have to depend on books to take in new ideas. Of course, using the Internet to search for information is also important. However, you just go on the Internet when you desperately need something in particular. Some digital information is difficult to find when needed, because I have stored a wealth of information in the computer. I think books are more valuable in this sense. However, if you really love books, you should make good use of them, instead of enshrining them on the shelf. Therefore, I love selecting books to gift others who really need them from time to time."

In September 2010, all the staff in Mr. Su's Studio traveled to Xi'an. It seems hard to imagine that employees from a small workshop in a second-tier Chinese city could have such a bonus trip. Since he left "*Fantasy*" magazine, Su has fully committed himself to his studio. When performing our duties as chief witnesses, Su said he had to go after exchanging a few words with me, claiming that the training for the studio was scheduled in the afternoon. "Training?" I was a little confused.

"Have you forgot that we used to have trainings on the weekend?" Su replied in smile. It was not until that moment that some pictures popped out in my mind: on a weekend afternoon, everyone was seated in a circle in the library which was walled by red bookshelves, talking about the interesting things taking place over the past week and looking through the newly arrived foreign books. Mr. Su would share with us some videos, and told us how to

apply certain techniques or deal with certain cases. It suddenly occurred to me that this tradition has survived in Su's studio for all the past years. Actually, Su likes to share with others. If you visit his blog from now and then, you will find new information and materials which you can download. Therefore, he has established a similar mechanism of "sharing" in his studio, hoping that every one will enjoy themselves through the "sharing" process.

"The word 'sharing' is equalized with 'happiness' in my vocabulary. I have come to this understanding little by little. For example, when you have just finished an illustration, you will feel fulfilled and happy. When you show it to others, you will find that the happiness is amplified. When standing on the Eiffel Tower and taking in the most breath-taking scenery in the world, I was a little sad rather than happy, because the one I love was not standing by my side. Therefore, you will feel an unprecedented sense of happiness when sharing with others. That trip to Xi'an made me happy. Every one in the studio wanted to go there, and they would find this trip rewarding. This decision has proven to be a right one."

The trip to Xi'an was a happy memory to Su, and also made him start to ask questions. It suddenly occurred to him that as a Chinese, his illustrations do not look Chinese at all.

"When I came back, I started to wonder whether there were too few Chinese elements in my works. During this trip, I had seen the awe-inspiring Terra Cotta Warriors, shadow puppet, and stele and inscriptions, all of which evidenced the greatness of the Chinese culture. I started to think about how to incorporate these Chinese elements into my illustrations, and integrate them with modern and cartoon arts. My illustrations used to feature few ethnic elements, not due to dislike but due to unfamiliarity with them. In the former passages, I mentioned that I liked novel things. In the first few years in my career, Western cartoon and comic works were absolutely new to me. Therefore, I had spent a lot of time searching for Western-style cartoons. Whenever others asked me of something featuring ethnic flavors, I didn't know what to do. Looking back now, it is true that I hadn't paid due attention to the ethnic elements. Of course, I am mostly commissioned by foreign clients, who would not ask me to draw somethig Chinese, maybe due to their inadequate understanding of our folk arts. Therefore, I had no chance to incorporate Chinese elements into my works." When discussing with the publisher about the title of this book, I still insisted on highlighting the notion of "American-style," because in this way, those in love of this particular style will easily locate this book among the flooding Japanese manga textbooks. In addition, we have always been engaged in bridging the gap between European and domestic character design industries. All the interviewees, net friends, clients, publishers and workshops are waiting for a book which can share with the Chinese designers the expertise and experience of European artists. Just like Su has said, he is driven by instincts and passions about this profession, without thinking too much about the responsibilities to promote the Chinese culture."

I paid a visit to Mr. Su last year. He had showed me two albums of illustrations. I thought they were titles by foreign publishers, because their qualities were superb. At last, he told me that these two albums were just his gift for himself, which were intended to showcase his commissions, as well as some extensive creations based on these commissions. It suddenly occurred to me that I should invite him to write a book, because I seldom find someone like him who can treat his hobby with such a professional attitude — he has spent over twenty years working on something that promises no commercial benefits, simply inspired by his unyielding passions.

"Haha! I was having a great fun! It is true that none of them has produced any commerical values. Maybe people living in this age are too eager to succeed. They are so result-oriented. I quite understand. Because they need money to pay for their house and vehicle. I am lucky that I'm doing something I like for a living. Actually, things that don't promise any commerical benefits are more beneficial than material benefits in the long term — is it a

little tricky?"

"Is there any category that you are not skilled enough to draw, or some kinds of commissions that you would like to turn down?" I started to dig more.

"Maybe the answer is things featuring the ethnic flavor. However, it is not because I can't draw them, but that I don't have the chance to practice. Nowadays, I have always heard the young designers complaining that they cannot do this or that, which will be followed by various excuses. It should be made clear in the first place that you are a professional rather than amateur. There is not such a notion of mission impossible for us. After all, you are required to construct a bridge on paper instead of in real life. When reviewing some commissions for the first time, I might wonder whether these concepts can be translated into concrete illustrations. However, based on my experience, I have full confidence that all the projects are feasible as long as I attach enough attention to them. Sometimes, artists will be faced with some commissions he doesn't like at all. For example, I once met with an Arabian-British, who wanted me to start from some drafts he finished by himself. I had tried my best to bring his works to a higher level. However, he asked me to return to his originals and start all over again. No designer likes such commissions, because you are only expected to work as tracer. I believe that man would find nobody who is willing to do that for him."

At last, we had started to talk about "dreams," in this age when people were too timid to talk about "dreams."

I have known Mr. Su for years, during which he has been playing different roles. The media tend to put a lot of titles before his name. However, all these titles can be summarized into a single identity "painter." In his own words, he has an inherent passion for painting. He doesn't know what else he can do except painting. Therefore, all his dreams are based on this passion. It suddenly occurred to me that life was just like traveling on the road. No matter he drives fast, and slowly, we are always by each other's side. We will not be intimidated by any challenge or any frenzied rivals, because we know it for

sure where we are heading for, and we never doubt that we will finally arrive at our destinations.

"Though it seems that I have been constantly changing my roles, from a freelancer to art director, from chief editor to commissioning editor, and then going back to run a studio. All these changes are driven by an earnest desire to translate my dreams into reality. I have never stepped back! When editing the magazine, I was concerned about how to move faster and faster, because media staff always have to race with time. We would be extremely occupied at the forthcoming holidays. The distribution work involved more difficulty. I had to worry about a lot of things. Now, I have detached myself from this exhausting job, and learn to slow down in my life. I even have the time to go shopping! It is kind of strange. Ever since I have stopped rushing around, all kinds of honors start to knock at the door. My works were selected into "Spectrum" and claimed EXPOSÈ Master Award. This year, my illustration album would be published in the United States. Some designers might have to try hard and wait for many years to make this happen. However, I have obtained this when I'm not expecting it. In this sense, it is true that one has to slow down in order to take in the scenery along the road. Don't regret that you have missed so much scenery when you are already aged." I'm so pleased that Su's book will come out in China, because he has waited for so long to share with the readers the scenery he has seen for himself in along the road.

Note: Dr. Henry Jekyll: the protagonist of Hollywood movie "Dr. Jekyll + Mr. Hyde," who will act as a doctor in the day but turns into a beast at night.

ACKNOWLEDGEMENT

This book is dedicated to my parents, who have not only brought me to this world, but also encouraged me to choose a profession which I'm really passionate about. I am so lucky, because I'm doing what I like for a living! I have finally made a character designer. This book is also dedicated to my beloved wife, who has offered me a lot of good suggestions as my first audience. My life would be as unaccomplished as a half-drawn draft without her support.

Meanwhile, I have to extend my sincere thanks to my friends Dean Yeagle, Stephen Silver, Florian Satzinger, Francisco Herrera and Ben Cadwell, whose impressive works are showcased in the fourth part of this book. I feel so honored that all these top character designers would like to make their contributions to this book.

Besides, I want to thank my Spanish friend Enrique Fernandez, even though due to time limitations, his works have not been presented in this book. He is one of the most outstanding character designers and the most t alented in this profession. His "The Wonderful Wizard of Oz" has always been one of my favorite.

In addition, I have to say thanks to my friend Tom Bancroft. As a successful Disney animator, he has authored the book "*Creating Characters with Personality*" and created Mushu in "*Mulan.*" Today, this book is enshrined as a bible on character design, which has helped me a lot when I am working on this book. Thank you, Tom!

I have to express my thanks to my yesterday's colleague and today's friend Vincent Zhao Yongquan. It is due to his earnest recommendations that this book has finally come out. In the end of this book is his interview with me, which is very special for me. He knows a lot about me and understands how to extract answers from me. You should not miss the interview.

Besides, I'm grateful for the supports and assistance from China Youth Press. Due to their marketing campaigns, this book is globally distributed in Chinese, English and French. I also owe much to the commissioning editor of this book, Yvonne Zhao. Her meticulous planning and scheduling work has helped me to finish this book step by step. In the later process, she has worked with other editorial staff to copy-edit and proof-read this book for many times to ensure an optimal structure and correct information.

At last, I have to say "thank you" to the staff of my studio. They have helped me to make revisions and finish the coloring work, which has saved me a lot of time and enabled me to immerse myself in an artists' paradise every day so that I can produce a better book.

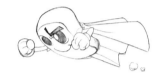

Alive Character Design: Character Design Course by Haitao Su

Authors: Haitao Su, Vincent Zhao

Project Editors: Guang Guo, Yvonne Zhao

English Editors: Fiona Wong, Dora Ding

Translator: Coral Yee

Copy Editor: Lee Perkins

Book Designer: Na Liu

© 2011 by China Youth Press, Roaring Lion Media Co., Ltd. and CYP International Ltd. China Youth Press, Roaring Lion Media Co., Ltd. and CYP International Ltd. have all rights which have been granted to CYP International Ltd. to publish and distribute the English edition globally.

First published in the United Kingdom in 2011 by CYPI PRESS.

Add: 79 College Road, Harrow Middlesex, HA1 1BD, UK

Tel: +44 (0) 20 3178 7279

Fax: +44 (0) 19 2345 0465

E-mail: sales@cypi.net editor@cypi.net

Website: www.cypi.co.uk

ISBN: 978-0-9562880-7-3

Printed in China